Intermediate Read about China

中国图符

Chinese Symbols and Icons

Richmond Public Library

列治文中文學校基金會

捐贈

Generously donated by
Richmond Chinese School Foundation

Copyright © 2009 The Commercial Press (H.K.) Ltd.
First Edition, January 2009

All rights reserved. No part of this publication may be reproduced or transmitted in any form or by any means, electronic or mechanical, including photocopying, recording, scanning, or any information storage or retrieval system, without written permission from the publisher.

Published by: The Commercial Press (U.S.) Ltd.
13-17 Elizabeth Street, 2nd Floor
New York, NY 10013

Chinese Symbols and Icons
Intermediate READ ABOUT CHINA

Editor: Catarina Wong

Printed in Hong Kong

http://www.chinese4fun.net

Contents
目 录

出 版 说 明　　Publisher's Note

一、十二生肖 1
　　The 12 Animal Signs of the Chinese Zodiac
　　GAMES FOR FUN

二、龙 11
　　The Dragon
　　Expansion Reading　The Dragon Boat Race
　　GAMES FOR FUN

三、凤 23
　　The Phoenix
　　Expansion Reading　A Hundred Birds Worshipping the Phoenix

四、太极图 33
Tai chi

> **Expansion Reading** The Legend of *Yin Yang* and the Invention of Binary Theory

GAMES FOR FUN

五、八卦 43
The Eight Trigrams

> **Expansion Reading** The Different Dual Combinations Formed from the Eight Trigrams

六、红双囍 54
Double Happiness

> **Expansion Reading** The Magpie and Happiness

GAMES FOR FUN

七、福 64
Good Fortune

> **Expansion Reading** The Custom of Hanging the Symbol for Fortune, Upside Down

GAMES FOR FUN

八、寿 74
Longevity

> **Expansion Reading** The Noodles of Longevity

GAMES FOR FUN

九、中国结 85
Chinese Knotting

Expansion Reading Some Common Chinese Knots

GAMES FOR FUN

十、门神 96
The Door Gods

Expansion Reading How Zhong Kui Became the Door God

十一、狮子 107
The Lion

Expansion Reading The Lion Dance

GAMES FOR FUN

十二、玉 119
Jade

Expansion Reading The Origin of the Jadeite Cabbage

PUBLISHER'S NOTE

After studying one to two years of Chinese you have also gained the knowledge of quite a bit of vocabulary. You may be wondering whether there are any other ways for you to further improve your Chinese language proficiency? Although there are a lot of books in the market that are written for people who are studying Chinese it is not easy to find an interesting and easy to read book that matches up to one's level of proficiency. You may find the content and the choice of words for some books to be too difficult to handle. You may also find some books to be too easy and the content is too naive for high school students and adults. Seeing the demand for this kind of learning materials we have designed a series of reading materials, which are composed of vivid and interesting content, presented in a multi-facet format. We think this can help students who are learning Chinese to solve the above problem. Through our reading series you can improve your Chinese and at the same time you will learn a lot of China culture.

Our series includes Chinese culture, social aspects of China, famous Chinese literary excerpts, pictorial symbols of

China, famous Chinese heroes…and many other indispensable aspects of China for those who want to really understand Chinese culture. While enjoying the reading materials one can further one's knowledge of Chinese culture from different angles. The content of the series are contextualized according to the wordbase categorization of HSK. We have selected our diction from the pre-intermediate, intermediate to advanced level of Chinese language learners. Our series is suitable for students at the pre-intermediate, intermediate to advanced level of Chinese and working people who are studying Chinese on their own.

The body of our series is composed of literary articles. The terms used in each article are illustrated with the romanised system called Hànyǔ pīnyīn for the ease in learning the pronunciation. Each article has an English translation with explanation of the vocabulary. Moreover there is related background knowledge in Expansion Reading. Interesting games are added to make it fun to learn. We aim at presenting a three-dimensional study experience of learning Chinese for our readers.

十二生肖
Shí èr shēngxiào

The 12 Animal Signs of the Chinese Zodiac

Pre-reading Questions

1. What are the purposes for creating 12 animal signs of the Chinese zodiac?
2. Why is the cat absent from the selected 12 animal signs?
3. What time in the year are the 12 animal signs most often seen in China?

---

❶ 中国人与十二生肖
Zhōngguórén yǔ shí èr shēngxiào

西方有十二星座[1]，中国有十二生肖。十二生肖由十二种动物组成。按顺序[2]排列分别是鼠、牛、虎、兔、龙、蛇、马、羊、猴、鸡、狗、猪。中国人一出生，就有一种动物作为自己的生肖。在中国古代用一种动物代表一年,十二年为一个周期。这十二种动物就是十二生肖。你出生那年的代表动物,就是你的生肖。在民间有很多关于十二生肖的故事,其中一个是这样的:传说天上的皇帝要举行竞赛,先到终点[3]的十二种动物,将会成为人间记录年的符号[4]。老鼠和猫不会游泳,便请牛帮忙。它们跳到牛的背上,一起过河。老鼠趁猫不注意,推了它下水。快到终点时,老鼠还跳到牛前面,得了第一名。于是,牛只得了第二名。其余的动物也陆续到达,成了十二生肖。

A coin with engraved Chinese zodiac signs

GLOSSARY

1 星座　the signs of the zodiac　　2 顺序　sequence; order; in proper order
3 终点　destination　　　　　　　　4 符号　a symbol; a mark

Translation

❶ The Chinese People and 12 Animal Signs of the Chinese Zodiac

In Western culture there are 12 zodiac signs, in Chinese astrology there are also twelve signs of the zodiac, which consists of 12 animals. The 12 animals appear in a cyclical order of the rat, the ox, the tiger, the rabbit, the dragon, the snake, the horse, the ram, the monkey, the rooster, the dog and the pig. Whenever a Chinese person is born he or she has an animal that symbolizes that category of years of his or her birth. In ancient China, a system of using one animal to represent each year was developed. They used a cyclical order of 12 animals respectively to record and label the chronological order of the years. Each cycle of 12 animals represents each chronological cycle of 12 years. The origin of these 12 birth sign animals is related to many folk stories. According to a legend, the Heavenly Emperor is conducting a race among all the animals. The first 12 animals that cross the finish line will become the 12 symbols for recording and labeling the chronological order of the years. The rat and the cat do not know how to swim and ask the ox for help. They jump on the back of the ox to cross the river. The rat uses the moment of opportunity when the cat is not paying any attention and pushes it into the river. When they are just about to reach the finish line the mouse jumps in front of the ox and becomes the first one that crosses the finish line and the ox can only earn the second place in the order of 12. Then the rest of the animals arrive one after the other forming the 12 animal signs.

❷ 十二生肖与性格特征

在中国古代，人与动物的关系非常密切。在日常生活中，人们观察动物的特点，并把它们和生肖的性格特点联系起来。人的生肖是哪种动物，或许[5]也会有类似的特点。比如，牛是中国农民的好助手，它一生辛勤耕种[6]，努力工作。有些人就认为生肖是牛的人也

Ox ploughing

勤劳、老实,能吃苦。那生肖是蛇的人会不会非常狡猾呢?有些中国人有另外一些看法。他们觉得蛇的外表[7]有点像龙,行动很冷静,能适应环境。于是他们想,生肖属蛇的人,也懂得解决问题,是有才能的人。十二生肖各有优点与缺点,并没有绝对好的或者绝对坏的生肖。也许你还有疑问。龙是想像出来的动物,它怎么会与人的生活有关系呢?在中国的传说中,龙可以给农作物[8]带来雨水[9],帮助耕种,所以传统中国人都喜欢龙,甚至崇拜[10]它。

GLOSSARY

5 或许　maybe
6 耕种　to farm
7 外表　appearance
8 农作物　agricultusral crops
9 雨水　rainfall
10 崇拜　worship

Translation

❷ The 12 Animal Signs of the Chinese Zodiac and the Personality Traits

In ancient China, people and animals were very closely related. In daily life people made observations of the animals. Special characteristics and traits of behavior were identified from these observations. The traits of a certain birth sign animal became the personality traits of that birth sign and then they were associated with people bearing that particular birth sign. When a person's birth sign had been identified maybe he or she had the personality traits of that birth sign animal. For instance the ox is a good helper of Chinese farmers. It works hard for its whole life, contributing to various agricultural activities. Some people may think that people bearing the birth sign of the ox are also hardworking, honest and have the ability to put up with hardships in life. Then by the same logic, should people bearing the birth sign of the snake be regarded as very cunning? Some Chinese people may look at the interpretation of this logic in a different way. They feel that the external appearance of a snake looks a bit like the dragon. It is cool and calm in behavior and can acclimatize to different circumstances. Then they think that people bearing the birth sign of a snake should also be similar to the snake in its capability to solve problems. They are capable people with talents. Each of the 12 animals of the 12 birth signs has its good traits and its shortcomings in personality. There is not a single birth sign animal, which is absolutely good or absolutely bad. Maybe you still have one more question. The dragon is an animal created out of the imagination of the people. How can it be related to the daily living of the ordinary people? In Chinese legends the dragon can bring rainfall for the cultivation of agricultural crops, helping the farmers. Traditionally, all Chinese people like the dragon. They even worship the dragon.

❸ 生活中的十二生肖

一年之中,最常会见到十二生肖图案[11]的时候,就是中国的农历[12]新年了。新年时,四处都可以看到该年的生肖图案或图片。不少商店或商场会以生肖图案做布置。很多新年图画和春联上也印有生肖的图案,吸引顾客买来做新年的装饰品。也有人会挑选与生肖有关的商品,当作新年礼物送给亲戚

Chinese zodiac stamp

朋友。有一类书，只会在接近新年或新年时才会出版。那就是谈生肖与运气的书籍。这些书预测[13]新一年不同生肖的人的运气，比如事业、爱情、健康等。就像有些人会注意自己的星座运气一样，很多中国人也希望知道新一年的生肖运气如何。

不过，有些人是不愿意说自己的生肖的。因为知道生肖代表的年份，便可以大概猜出年龄了。不想别人知道自己年龄的人，生肖自然是他们的秘密了！

GLOSSARY

11 图案　pattern
12 农历　the lunar calendar
13 预测　to predict; to forecast

Translation

❸ The 12 Animal Signs in Daily Living

　　Within the span of one year the Festival of the Chinese lunar New Year is the time that patterns of drawings of the 12 birth sign animals can most often be seen. During that period of time, patterns and pictures of the birth sign animal symbolizing that year can be seen everywhere. That particular animal appears as part of the in-store decorations on New Year pictures and red paper cuttings with Chinese characters symbolizing good fortune. These are used to attract customers to buy them as Chinese lunar New Year ornaments. There are also people who will select merchandises related to the birth sign animals as gifts for friends and relatives.

　　There are particular kinds of books, which are only published during the Chinese lunar New Year period. The books give the good and bad predictions for different people of all the 12 birth signs of that particular year. These books make predictions of the people of the 12 birth signs in their respective businesses or careers, romances and health etc. In western culture, people read their horoscopes to find out about their future. In the same way, Chinese people hope to know what luck will bring according to predictions related to their birth signs and relative to the birth sign of that particular year. But some people are unwilling to tell other people their birth signs because with the knowledge of one's birth sign one's age can be estimated from the 12-year cycle pattern. Naturally for people who are unwilling to reveal their age their birth signs are their secrets!

GAMES FOR FUN

Regarding the 12 birth sign animals Chinese people have created quite a few associations between the personality traits of the 12 animals and people with those respective signs. Can you match the special characteristics of the following animals with the personality traits, which the Chinese think to be the resemblances of those animals?

- a. Conscientious
- b. Sympathetic
- c. Inspirational, fickle
- d. Gentle, compassionate
- e. Persuasive
- f. Honest and direct
- g. Adaptive, smart
- h. Adventurous
- i. Energetic, self-assured
- j. Outgoing, impulsive
- k. Smart, sociable
- l. Reliable, just

12 kinds of animals

Answer:
Rat g / Ox a / Tiger h / Rabbit b / Dragon i / Snake c / Horse j / Ram d / Monkey k / Rooster e / Dog l / Pig f

Lóng
龙
The Dragon

Pre-reading Questions

1. In your imagination, What kind of animal do you think a dragon is?
2. Can you find the shadows of other animals on the body of the dragon?
3. Where have you seen the dragon as a picture symbol? Why does the dragon appear at those places?

---

❶ Lóng shì shénme
龙 是 什么？

Tán dào lóng nǐ kěnéng huì xiǎngqi yī zhī fùzé
谈 到 龙，你 可能 会 想起 一 只 负责
kānshǒu bǎozàng de dòngwù Tā sìzhī cūdà yǒu yī shuāng
看守¹ 宝藏² 的 动物。它 四肢³ 粗大⁴，有 一 双
chìbǎng kǒu zhōng pēn huǒ Zǒngzhī tāmen de yàngzi zǒngshì
翅膀，口 中 喷 火。总之，它们 的 样子 总是
xiōngbābā de yīdiǎnr yě bù yǒushàn shì xié'è de
凶巴巴⁵ 的，一点儿 也 不 友善，是 邪恶⁶ 的
dòngwù Zhè shì Ōuzhōu gùshi de lóng Zhōngguórén de lóng
动物。这 是 欧洲 故事 的 龙。中国人 的 龙

却是善良[7]的,是吉祥[8]的象征。中国人相信,龙是管理水的神。它有神力,懂得飞天入海,控制云和雨。相信你也认得中国龙的样子,但如果要你画一条龙,却不容易。

从古至今,中国的龙有很多不同的样子,有的像蛇,有的像虫[9],有的像鱼。直到北宋(公元960年至1127年)时,有画家提出[10]两个标准,龙才有了今天的样子。第一个标准是由头至

The Nine Dragon Wall, Beijing

jǐng yóu jǐng zhì fù、yóu
颈、由 颈 至 腹、由
fù zhì wěi sān bùfen de
腹 至 尾 三 部分 的
chángdù dàzhì xiāngtóng érqiě
长度 大致 相同，而且
hái yǒu cūxì de biànhuà Dì
还 有 粗细 的 变化。第
èr gè biāozhǔn shì lóng yǔ jiǔ
二 个 标准 是 龙 与 九
zhǒng dòngwù zhǎng de xiāngsì
种 动物 长 得 相似：
lóng de jiǎo xiàng lù、tóu xiàng
龙 的 角 像 鹿、头 像
luòtuo、yǎn xiàng tùzi、jǐng
骆驼、眼 像 兔子、颈
xiàng shé、fùbù de jiǎ xiàng
像 蛇、腹部 的 甲 像
yī gè yī gè dà hǎi bèi、lín xiàng yú、zhuǎ xiàng yīng
一 个 一 个 大 海 贝、鳞[11] 像 鱼、爪 像 鹰[12]、
zhǎng xiàng hǔ、ěrduo xiàng niú。Ànzhào zhèxiē biāozhǔn，nǐ
掌[13] 像 虎，耳朵 像 牛。按照 这些 标准，你
xiànzài dǒngde huà Zhōngguó lóng le ma
现在 懂得 画 中国 龙 了 吗？

The Dragon Wall, Shanghai

The dragon gate at San Francisco Chinatown

GLOSSARY

1	看守	to guard; to watch	2	宝藏	a treasury
3	四肢	the four limbs	4	粗大	thick and big
5	凶巴巴	fierce	6	邪恶	evil; wicked
7	善良	gentle; kind	8	吉祥	auspicious; propitious
9	虫	an insect; an worm	10	提出	to suggest; to bring up (an idea)
11	鳞	the scales	12	鹰	an eagle
13	掌	a palm			

Translation

❶ What is the Dragon?

When you talk about the dragon, you probably think of an animal responsible for the guarding of a treasure trove. Its four limbs are big and strong. It has a pair of wings and spits fire from its mouth. In short, its appearance is fearsome looking. It does not show even a little bit of friendliness and is an evil animal. This is the dragon in European stories. But the dragon as conceived by the Chinese people is kind and gentle, a symbol of good fortune. The Chinese people believe that the dragon is the god which takes care of the water. It has the supernatural power. It knows how to fly in the sky and to swim deep in the ocean. It controls the formation of the clouds and the rain. I believe you may be able to recognize a Chinese dragon. But it is not an easy task if you have to draw one.

From ancient times till now the Chinese Dragon has had a lot of different appearances. Some dragons look like snakes and some look like worms, or fish. Until the Northern Song Dynasty (960 – 1127 A.D.) a painter suggested two criteria for drawing the dragon, which then allowed the dragon to evolve into how it appears modern times. The first criterion is the approximately equal measurements in the length of the three sections of the body, namely from the head to the neck, from the neck to the abdomen, and from the abdomen to the tail. Also the variations in thickness cross-section-wise have been specified. The second criterion specifies the appearances of the nine body parts of the dragon with nine kinds of animals. Its horns should look like those of a deer; its head should look like that of a camel; its eyes should look like those of a rabbit; its neck should look like that of a snake; each of its abdominal amour-like skin covering should look like a big sea shell; its scales should look like those of a fish; its claws should look like those of an eagle; its paws should look like those of a tiger; its ears should look like those of an ox. According to these criteria do you know how to draw a Chinese dragon now?

❷ 究竟 中国人 认为 龙 是 怎样 的 动物？

龙 能够 上 天，与 天 联系；龙 能够 飞，有 超越[14] 困难 的 意思；龙 喜欢 水，水 对 生命 很 重要。中国 古代 是 农业 社会，重视 雨水。龙 有 掌管[15] 云 和 雨 的 能力，因此 认为 龙 是 保护 神，大家 相信 江 河 湖 海 都 有 龙，不 下 雨 的 时候，就 向 龙 求 雨。佛教 和 道教 的 故事 里 常常 出现 海龙王。后来，因为 皇帝 喜欢 龙，皇宫[16] 中 有 很多 龙 的 装饰。龙 成为 皇帝 用 的 图案，龙 也 变成

The ocean dragon king

Dragon ornament on the roof

15

了皇帝的象征：皇帝穿的是龙袍[17]，坐的是龙椅，睡的是龙床。不过，中国老百姓也喜欢龙，只是他们用的龙不能和皇帝用的一样。

现在没有皇帝了，龙高高在上[18]的感觉已经减少，但中国人仍然喜欢龙，因为它给人积极、刚强、朝气[19]、吉祥的感觉。

Dragon robe worn by Qing Emperor

GLOSSARY

14 超越　to surpass, to transcend
15 掌管　be in charge of; to control
16 皇宫　(imperial) palace
17 袍　robe; gown
18 高高在上　in a prominent position
19 朝气　vigor; vitality; youthful spirit

Translation

❷ **What Kinds of Animals are in the Minds of Chinese People when they are Thinking of the Dragon?**

The dragon is related to Heaven because it can get up there; its ability to fly conveys the meaning that it can surpass difficulties; the dragon likes water, which is very important to the support of life as a whole. The agricultural society in ancient China put a very heavy emphasis on rainfall. Since the dragon has the supernatural ability to control and command the formation of the clouds and the rain, people think that it is their god of protection. People believe that dragons exist in all the rivers, lakes and oceans. When it does not rain people plead to the dragon for rain. Ocean dragon kings frequently appear in the religious stories of Buddhism and Taoism. Later on because of the emperors' liking of the dragon, a lot of dragon-like designs were used in the imperial palace. Those designs became the royal ones used exclusively for the emperors. The dragon became the symbol of the emperors. The robe worn by an emperor was a dragon robe. The chair on which he sat was a dragon chair. The bed on which he slept was a dragon bed. But the ordinary people of China also liked the dragon. However, the dragon designs they used could not be the same as those of the emperors.

Now there are no more emperors in China and the aloof feeling of the associated image of the dragon-emperor being in a prominent position has decreased. But the Chinese still love the dragon because it gives people the feeling of being positive, strong, full of lively energy and being in a state of grace and fortune.

❸ 生活中的龙

自从龙从皇宫走进平民[20]的生活后，在中国很容易可以找到龙的影子。龙出现在不少著名故事里。例如在故事《柳毅传书》中，有海龙王的女儿与一个读书人的爱情故事；在《西游记》里，海龙王将龙宫里的一根大柱子送了给孙悟空做武器，那就是大家都认识的"金箍棒"；成语"画龙点睛"的

Dragon boat race

故事,讲一个画家在墙上画了一条龙,因为画得太似,当画家为龙点上眼睛后,就变成有生命,飞往天上。现在中国仍然有很多关于龙的习俗[21],像舞龙和龙船比赛。舞龙是新年或重要活动的节目。划龙船比赛则在农历五月五日的端午节举行,这是纪念诗人屈原的节日。龙船的样子很像一条龙,每艘龙船可以坐很多人。比赛开始后,多艘龙船一同斗快划向终点。

GLOSSARY

20 平民　the common people; the populace
21 习俗　a custom; a convention

Translation

❸ The Dragon in Our Daily Lives

    Since the dragon has emerged from the imperial palace and has entered into the daily life of the ordinary people one can easily find its shadows in China. It appears in quite a few famous stories. For instance the romantic novel, *Liu yi and the Dragon Princess* tells the love story between a scholar and the daughter of an ocean dragon king. In the mythological novel, *Journey to the West* an ocean dragon king gives a giant pillar of the dragon palace to Sun Wukong, the monkey king, as a gift so that he can make a weapon out of it. This is the "*Jingu Bang*", with which everyone is familiar. The idiom, "The final and crucial touch on the eye of the dragon", comes from a story, in which a painter painted a dragon on the wall. Because the painting was so vivid and realistic when the final touch was painted on the eye it became alive and flew up into Heaven. In modern China there are still a lot of customs related to the dragon, like the dragon dance and the dragon boat race. The dragon dance is one of the items on the agenda of the Chinese lunar New Year and other important social activities. The dragon boat race takes place on the fifth day of the fifth month of the Chinese lunar calendar. It is called The Duanwu Festival, the day set aside to remember Qu Yuan, the poet. A dragon boat looks like a dragon. Each dragon boat can sit many people. After the race begins, many dragon boats race toward the finish line.

The Dragon Boat Race – Commemorating the Poet Qu Yuan

The duanwu festival is on the fifth day of the fifth lunar month. This festival began in memory of Qu Yuan, the great ancient Chinese poet.

Qu Yuan was a government official of the State of Chu in the Warring States period. Emperor Chu Huaiwang not only refused to listen to Qu Yuan's plan to change the laws in order to strengthen the nation but he also dismissed Qu Yuan, sending him into exile far away from the capital. On his way to exile he wrote many famous poems expressing his concerns about the people.

Rice dumplings

Later on, the State of Qin attacked the State of Chu and captured her capital. Qu Yuan felt that all hope had been shattered and on the fifth day of the fifth lunar month in 278 B.C. he committed suicide and died for his nation by jumping into the Miluo River (in the southern part of the City of Changsha: Hunan Province, in modern times).

According to the legend, when the local people heard of this news they felt so painfully sad that they rowed their boats, racing to the place of the suicide trying to rescue him. (Unfortunately, they were unable to recover his body.) They could not bear the thought of Qu Yuan's body being eaten up by the fish so they threw rice dumplings into the river to feed the fish.

Later on, this attempt to rescue Qu Yuan by boat is commemorated in the annual dragon boat race. The custom of eating rice dumplings at the Duanwu festival reflects the people's sympathetic act of throwing rice dumplings into the river to feed the fish to prevent Qu Yuan's body from being eaten.

GAMES FOR FUN

Which of the following animals have body parts that resemble those of a dragon? Can you circle them?

Deer

Fish

Ram

Pig

Elephant

Snake

Ox

Eagle

Rooster

Answer:
Deer / Fish / Snake / Eagle

Fèng
凤
The Phoenix

Pre-reading Questions

1. Why are the dragon and the phoenix often appearing together?
2. How much do you know about the things that have the dragon and the phoenix appearing together? Does the phoenix represent male or female?

---

❶ 亲密[1] 的 凤 与 龙
Qīnmì de fèng yǔ lóng

在 中国, 看 到 龙 的 地方, 常常 也 可以
Zài Zhōngguó kàn dào lóng de dìfang chángcháng yě kěyǐ

看 到 凤。龙 和 凤 经常 是
kàn dào fèng. Lóng hé fèng jīngcháng shì

一对。为什么 这 两 种 不同
yīduì. Wèishénme zhè liǎng zhǒng bùtóng

的 动物 会 在 一起 呢?
de dòngwù huì zài yīqǐ ne?

凤 和 龙 一样, 都 是
Fèng hé lóng yīyàng, dōu shì

吉祥 的 动物。凤 是 所有
jíxiáng de dòngwù. Fèng shì suǒyǒu

Phoenix ornament on the roof of a temple

鸟类的王。鸟能够飞,所以古代的人崇拜鸟。这些会飞的神奇[2]动物,应该有个领袖。于是,人便想像出凤。凤既然是鸟王,它的样子和本领一定超过所有鸟类,它应该比任何一种鸟更美丽,更大。我们看见的凤,头上有冠[3],眼睛尖而长,尾巴有长长的美丽羽毛[4]。凤集合了不同鸟类的特征,成为最美丽的鸟。凤可以在空中飞,它飞的姿态很优美。凤喜欢唱歌,它的声音很好听。凤又喜欢太阳,画家常常画一只凤面向太阳的画。

凤与龙都具有强大的力量,地位都很崇高。最初可能有些人崇拜龙,有些人崇拜凤。后来两群人合起来,同时崇拜龙和凤。龙与凤在一起,互相配合,是和谐的象征。

GLOSSARY

1 亲密 close; intimate
2 神奇 magical; miraculous
3 冠 a crown; a crest
4 羽毛 feather

Translation

❶ The Intimately Related Pair, the Phoenix and the Dragon

In China wherever you see a dragon you frequently find a phoenix. They often appear in pairs. Why are these two different kinds of animals put together?

Like the dragon, the phoenix is also an animal of good fortune. The phoenix is the king of all birds. Birds can fly. Therefore ancient people worshipped birds. They thought that these supernatural creatures that could fly should have a leader. This was how and why the image of the phoenix was conceived. Since the phoenix was the king of all the birds its appearance and abilities must surpass all the birds. It should be prettier and bigger than any bird. The phoenix, which we see nowadays, has a crown. Her eyes are long and narrow. Her tail is composed of extra long and beautiful feathers. The image of the phoenix is a composite of the special characteristics of different kinds of birds. It has become the most beautiful bird. The phoenix can fly in the sky and its flying movements are very graceful. The phoenix likes to sing. Its voice is very pleasant to the ears. The phoenix also likes the sun. Painters frequently paint a phoenix facing the sun in their pictures.

Both the phoenix and the dragon have strong power and their positions command very high esteem. In the beginning some people might worship only the dragon. Some might only worship the phoenix. Later on both groups combined together to worship both the dragon and the phoenix at the same time because when they are put together they are a complementary pair, which is a symbol of harmony.

❷ 凤是女，龙是男？

本来龙和凤都有公有母。凤和凰才是真的一对，凤是公的，凰是母的，所以这种鸟中之王又叫做凤凰。凤要找妻子，叫做凤求凰。老子曾经把孔子比喻为凤，皇帝也喜欢用凤来代表自己，可见凤和龙一样，本来都代表值得尊重的男性。那么，为什么后来的人又会用凤代表女性呢？

Phoenix coronet of a Qing Empress

原来从唐朝（公元618年至907年）开始，皇帝便习惯只用龙作为象征。龙与凤

Phoenix coronet for Chinese opera

配合代表和谐,因此,皇后就用凤作为象征。皇后穿的礼服、戴的帽子上,都有凤的图案。从此,凤与龙在一起时,龙便代表男,凤则代表女。

龙和凤一起代表了两种不同的美好事物结合在一起,配合得刚刚好。龙凤结合的图案,叫做龙凤呈祥。

A phoenix coronet

Translation

❷ Is the Phoenix the Female and is the Dragon, therefore, the Male?

Originally both the Dragon and the Phoenix have their own male and female sexual corresponding partners of their own kinds. The *feng* and the *huang* are the real pair in the Phoenix category. The *feng* is the male and the *huang* is the female. Therefore these birds as a group are collectively regarded as the King of all birds and are called *fenghuang*. When a *feng* looks for a wife it is called a *feng* courting a *huang*. At one time Laozi compared Confucius with a phoenix. Emperors also liked to use the phoenix to represent themselves. You can see that the phoenix was the same in social hierarchy as the Dragon. Originally they both represented respectable men. Then why was the phoenix used later on to represent the female?

It originated in the Tang dynasty (618–907 A.D.). From habit, the emperors used only the dragon as their symbol. Since the complementary pairing of the dragon and the phoenix represents harmony, the empresses then used the phoenix as their symbol. Then the designs of the phoenix appeared on the ceremonial apparel and the hats worn by the empresses. From then on when the dragon is put together with the phoenix the former represents the male and the latter represents the female.

The juxtaposition of the dragon and the phoenix represents the integration of two different kinds of good and beautiful things. They complement each other just perfectly. The design showing the integration of the dragon and the phoenix is called "*longfeng cheng xiang*", the auspicious sign manifested by the integration of the dragon and the phoenix.

❸ 民间的凤

自从龙与凤分了性别，龙凤在一起不仅代表和谐与吉祥，还象征爱情。因此，在婚礼上常常见到龙凤图案。这个图案的意思是，这对夫妻就像龙凤一样，能互相配合，补充对方的不足，是彼此最好的对象。生活上协调[5]得很好，婚姻也很幸福。新娘[6]的礼服上有凤的装饰。从前戴冠

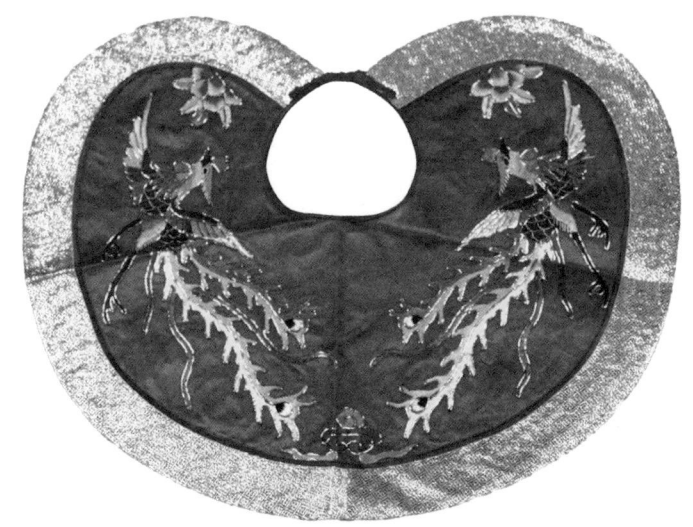

A bridal phoenix wardrobe

29

的时候，新娘戴的冠和皇后的冠一样，称为凤冠。

除了结婚，生孩子也是一个家庭重要的喜事。[7] 如果一胎刚好生了一男一女的双生儿，[8] 叫做龙凤胎，[9] 中国人认为是很难得的。父母都希望自己的儿女能成功、健康。所以就有了"望子成龙"和"望女成凤"的说法。意思就是盼望儿子能像龙一样，女儿则像凤一样，成为品德和成就都很高的人。

A red packet with dragon and phoenix design

GLOSSARY

5 协调　coordinate; harmonize
6 新娘　bride
7 喜事　happy event; joyous occasion
8 双生儿　twins
9 龙凤胎　twins (a boy and a girl)

Translation

❸ The Phoenix among Ordinary Folks

    Ever since the dragon and the phoenix have been divided into their respective sexual roles, the juxtaposition of the dragon and the phoenix not only represents harmony and good fortune. It also symbolizes love. Therefore the design with the juxtaposition of the dragon and the phoenix can frequently be seen at weddings. The meaning of this design is that this couple of husband and wife is like the perfect match of the dragon and the phoenix. They can complement each other, their good points covering up the others' shortcomings. They are the best courtship partners of each other and they coordinate very well in their daily living. Their marriage too is going to be very happy. The ceremonial apparel of the brides is decorated with the design of the phoenix. In previous times, when people wore crowns, the crowns worn by the bride were the same as the one worn by the Empress. They were called the *Feng guan*, the phoenix crown. Besides getting married, bearing children is also an important and happy affair of the family. If twins, who are a boy and a girl, are born they are called a *longfeng tai*, a dragon and phoenix twins. The Chinese people think that *longfeng tai* is hard to get and therefore precious. All parents hope their children can become successful and healthy. Therefore there are sayings like *wang zi cheng long*, wishing a son to become a dragon and *wang nü cheng feng*, wishing a daughter to become a phoenix. They both mean that the parents want their sons and the daughters to grow up to become mature adults as morally ethical as the dragon and the phoenix with very high achievements in society.

Expansion Reading

A Hundred Birds Worshipping the Phoenix

Can you imagine the scene of one hundred birds gathering at the same time? It must be spectacular! Among the ancient Chinese legends there is this story of one hundred birds worshipping the phoenix at the same time. Why did over one hundred birds come to worship the phoenix?

The legendary phoenix was the king of birds and lived high up on a tall mountain. Every year around the time of the mid-autumn festival, over a hundred birds would come to the mountain to pay their respects to their king, the phoenix. One year when the phoenix

Phoenix decoration in a Chinese restaurant

and the birds were happily singing and flying around dancing, large snowflakes suddenly fell from the sky. The temperature dropped rapidly with chilling winds blowing right against the faces of the birds, which were shivering in the cold. At this moment the phoenix plucked out all its beautiful feathers and distributed them to the birds helping them to fight the cold weather and to escape from it. After the hundred birds left, the snow collected on the ground became even thicker and the winds blew even stronger. Without feathers to fight the cold weather and to fly, the phoenix was frozen alive and consequently died. On every commemorative day of the death of the phoenix, a hundred birds would gather on the mountain to express their condolences and sing sadly to express their grief about the death of the Phoenix.

The self-sacrificial act of the phoenix to save a hundred birds deeply moved the people, who afterwards regarded the phoenix as a bird of high moral ethics.

Tàijí tú
Tai chi

Pre-reading Questions

1. Where have you seen the picture symbol of *tai chi*?
2. What do you associate this picture symbol with?
3. Why is the *tai chi* symbol composed of the black and the white colors?

---

❶ Tàijí yǔ yīn yáng
太极 与 阴 阳

Zài Zhōngguó, chángcháng jiàndào zhège yóu hēisè hé
在 中国， 常常 见到 这个 由 黑色 和
báisè zǔchéng de tú'àn, zhège jiàozuò Tàijítú. Zài
白色 组成 的 图案， 这个 叫做 太极图。 在
Dàojiào sìmiào¹、 xuéxí
道教 寺庙¹、 学习
Tàijíquán² de dìfang huò
太极拳² 的 地方 或
fēngshuǐ yòng de bāguà
风水 用 的 八卦
shang, dōu kěyǐ zhǎodào
上， 都 可以 找到

Tai chi Symbol on the door of a martial art studio

33

太极图。有些人甚至用太极图案做成食物或饰物[3]等。

太极是表现世界刚刚形成的状态。中国人认为宇宙的最初像一团鸡蛋黄色的气体,慢慢地,当轻的气体向上[4]升,就变成天;重的气体向下[5]沉,就变成地。宇宙从此分了天和地,形成阳和阴,就像太极图的白色和黑色那样。

中国人认为世界是由"阴"和"阳"组成的。阳表示面向太阳,阴表示背向太阳。阴和阳表示各种相对的事物,例如:地对天、月与日、寒对热等。虽然阴和阳是相对的,但它们又是互相依靠的。就好像白天对黑夜一样。如果没有黑夜,就感受不到白天的光亮。黑夜完结,白天才会来临,所以

| báitiān | hé | hēiyè | jìshì | xiāngduì | yòu | shì | hùxiāng | yīkào | de |

白天和黑夜既是相对，又是互相依靠的。

GLOSSARY

1 寺庙　temple
2 太极拳　a kind of Chinese martial art
3 饰物　an ornaments; a decorations
4 向上　upward
5 向下　downward

Translation

❶ *Tai chi* and *Yin Yang*

In China one can oftn see a black and white symbol, called the *tai chi* symbol. It can be found in the Taoist temples, those places where people practice *tai chi chuan*, or on an eight-trigram compass board used in Feng Shui (the Chinese form of geomancy). Even food and ornaments have been made in the shape of this symbol.

Tai chi symbolises the condition when the world was formed. The Chinese think that the universe in the beginning stage looked like a big lump of gas with egg yolk-like color. Gradually, the lighter gas ascended upward and formed the sky and the heavier gas sank downward and became the earth. From then on the universe was divided into the sky and the earth just like the black and the white colour composition forming the *yinyang* combination in the *tai chi* symbol.

The Chinese think that the world is composed of the *yin* and the *yang*. The *yang* faces the sun and the yin backs away from the sun. This *yin yang* dichotomy represents various phenomena that have two opposing components. For example, the earth versus the sky; the moon versus the sun; cold versus heat. Although the *yin* and the *yang* oppose each other they also complement each other. Take the example of the day night dichotomy. If there were no "darkness" during the night one would not be able to feel the "brightness" during the day. The end of the night is the beginning of the day. So night and day oppose and complement each other.

❷ 阴阳生出万物

太极图简要地表示了阴阳和世界的关系。黑色的部分表示阴，白色的部分表示阳。黑白两半[6]，好像两条小鱼。两条小鱼虽然颜色不同，但形状一模一样[7]，好像双生儿，互相依靠。阴和阳代表了世界万物[8]不是单独存在的，就像女对男、水对火、暗与明，它们既对立，又亲密。

仔细看太极图，会发现白色部分有一个小黑点，而黑色部分又有一个小白点。这两个小圆点说明世界万物是没有绝对的黑或白的。小白点好像黑夜完结，太阳升[9]

Tai chi Sword

起来的第一道光。当光愈来愈多,就变成白天,即是白色部分的诞生。正如冬天完结才有春天,满月之后就会月缺[10]一样。世界由阴生出阳,阳生出阴,永不停止。当太极生出了阴和阳之后,便由阴和阳生出世界上所有的东西了。还不明白?试想想阴和阳就好像计算机原理中0和1,1和0组合起来,可以产生千变万化[11]的组合呢。

A woman playing Tai chi sword

GLOSSARY

6 两半　two halves
7 一模一样　exactly the same
8 万物　all things on earth
9 升　to rise
10 月缺　an ecliptic moon
11 千变万化　ever changing

Translation

❷ All Things on Earth is Derived from *Yin* and *Yang*

    The *tai chi* symbol has simplified the relationship between the *yin yang* dichotomy and the world. The white part represents the *yang* and the black part represents the *yin*. The two halves of the symbol are like two fish. Their colors are different but their appearances are the same. They are like a pair of twins leaning against each other. This *yin yang* binary concept symbolizes that every object in the world does not exist alone by itself. For instance, the male versus the female, fire versus water and darkness versus brightness in the demonstrated binary relationship. They are contradictory and yet very close to each other.

    On careful scrutiny of the *tai chi* symbol one will discover a small black dot in the white portion and a corresponding white one in the black portion. These two dots illustrate that nothing is absolutely black or white. The white dot can be compared to the first ray of the rising sun that ends the night. When the white light gets brighter and brighter it represents that the night has become the day. When the white fully shows itself the white part of the symbol is "born" in full. The same logic can be applied to the seasonal change that the end of the winter brings the beginning of the spring and a full moon always follows an ecliptic moon. The world operates on a gradually alternating and never ending metamorphosis between the *yin* and the *yang*. This *yin* and *yang* model derived from the *tai chi* symbol logic can be applied to everything and every phenomenon in the world. To understand this philosophy one can compare it to the computer logic of the binary digits of the 0 and the 1. Numerous combinations can be formed from this simple combination.

❸ 生活中的阴阳

中国人认为如果阴和阳配合，关系和谐，就是最好的状态。这个想法影响了中国的思想和文化。例如：中医认为人的体质和食物的性质分寒和热。寒是阴，热是阳。身体是寒性的人不适宜[12]吃寒性的食物，应该吃一些热性食物。而中性[13]的食物所有人都适合吃。中国人认为吃与身体配合的食物，可以治病[14]，这种想法叫做"医食同源"。中国书法也讲阴阳配合。黑字是阴，白纸是阳。黑字和白色的空间配合得好，才算是好书法。建筑方面，可以在紫禁城找到阴阳配合的例子。紫禁城是以前的皇宫，今天叫做故宫博物院。紫禁城里皇帝工作

People playing tai chi chuan

和 居住 的 建筑物，以 单数 为主，而皇后 和 妃子 的 住所 则 以 双数 为主。这 反映 了 中国 的 阴阳 观念 中，男性 是 阳，女性 是 阴；单数 是 阳，双数 是 阴 的 想法。从 阴阳 的 思想 中，可以 明白 中国人 是 十分 重视 人 和 自然 的 和谐 关系 的。

GLOSSARY

12 适宜 suitable; appropriate
13 中性 neutral
14 治病 to cure diseases

Translation

❸ *Yin Yang* in Everyday Life

The Chinese also think that the condition is at its best when the *yin* and the yang harmoniously coexist. This concept has a great deal of influence on the Chinese culture and philosophy. For example in traditional Chinese medicine the nature of the people and the food is classified into two categories, the "cold", and the "hot". The "cold" category is the *yin* in nature and the "hot" category is the *yang* in nature. People who are classified as "cold" in nature should not eat "cold" food. They should consume "hot" food. "Neutral" food is suitable for consumption by everyone. The Chinese believe that eating complementary food can cure diseases. This philosophy is called *yi shi tong yuan* meaning that food and medicines are both from the same source, Nature. The same *yin-yang* harmonious philosophy has also been applied to Chinese calligraphy. The black characters are the *yin* and the white space is the *yang*. A good illustration of Chinese calligraphy is when the black and white combination exists in harmony. Another example can be found in the architectural design of the Forbidden City. The former imperial palace, which has been renamed as Imperial Palace Museum. In the architectural design the number of offices and the residences of the emperor amount to an odd number whereas the corresponding number of the Empress and the concubines is an even number. This reflects the Chinese *yin-yang* conceptualisation. The male and the odd number are the *yang* and the female and the even number are the *yin*. These philosophical manifestations of the *yin-yang* dichotomy illustrate the high regards the Chinese have for the harmonious coexistence between the people and Nature.

The Legend of *Yin Yang* and the Invention of Binary Theory

We are aware of the philosophical similarity between the Chinese belief that the birth of everything in the world was from the *yin* and the *yang*, and the logical binary system of the two digits, the "0" and the "1". There has been speculation by some people, that there a relationship between the *yin-yang* belief and the binary system. Gottfried Wilhelm Leibniz was the original inventor of the binary system. He was also very interested in the culture of China. As an inventor he worked to invent a set of multiplication machines. After many years of research he finally finished the manuscript on the thesis of the binary system. The only thing was that it had not yet been published. He wrote to his good friend, Joachim Bouvet, to tell him his theory of how the binary system operated. At that time Joachim Bouvet, a French missionary, was in China teaching and spreading his religion. He hoped that he could introduce this theory of calculation to the Chinese Emperor, Kangxi. Joachim Bouvet wrote back to Gottfried Wilhelm Leibniz and told him that according to what Kangxi said, there was a similar school of thought in China. Then the Chinese Book of Change, the *I Ching*, and the theory of the *yin* and the *yang* were introduced by Joachim Bouvet to Gottfried Wilhelm Leibniz.

Afterwards, Gottfried Wilhelm Leibniz continued to improve on the theory of the binary system. Finally it became the theoretical basis of our modern day computers. Although no evidence can be found to prove any relationship between the *yin-yang* philosophical school of thought and binary theory, yet we can see that similar concepts exist both in the West and in China. The ancient Chinese concept of the *yin* and the *yang* had developed a lot earlier than its corresponding theory in the West.

GAMES FOR FUN

Which of the following belong to the *yin* and *yang* respectively? Can you circle those belong the *yin* with a red pen and *yang* with a blue pen?

Answer:

The representations of the *yin*:
Dark night, the earth or ground, move or active, a mother, a daughter or a girl, cold, winter, water, even numbers.

The representations of the *yang*:
A bright day, the sky, a father, a man or male, hot or heat, summer, fire, silence or silent, odd numbers.

Bāguà
八卦
The Eight Trigrams

Pre-reading Questions

1. Can you guess what are the uses of the Eight Trigrams?
2. What do the Chinese people believe about the relationships between the Eight Trigrams and *fengshui* (the study of Geomancy)?

---

❶ Shénme shì bāguà?
什么 是 八卦?

Yǒu yīxiē Zhōngguórén de fángzi wàimiàn, guà zhe yī
有 一些 中国人 的 房子 外面, 挂 着 一
miàn bājiǎoxíng de xiǎo jìngzi. Zhè bù shì zhuāngshìpǐn. Zhè
面 八角形 的 小 镜子。这 不 是 装饰品。这
miàn jìngzi jiàozuò bāguà jìng, shì
面 镜子 叫做 "八卦 镜", 是
yòng lái bìxié de. Wéirào zhe
用 来 避邪[1] 的。围绕 着
jìngzi de tú'àn, dōu yóu zhíxiàn
镜子 的 图案, 都 由 直线
zǔchéng, zhèxiē tú'àn jiàozuò
组成, 这些 图案 叫做

A bagua mirror

八卦。别小看这些简单的图案,里面包含了中国重要的思想。

传说八卦是中国的祖先伏羲画的,后来《易经》记载了这八个图。《易经》是中国最古老的占卜[2]书,八卦是占卜用的。《易经》认为世界的事物都在变化,人应该留意。易就是变化、变易的意思,所以不读做容易的易。

据孔子解释《易经》,世界本来是一团气体,由一变二,就是阴和阳,再由二变四,四变八。八就是八卦。八卦可以代表八种自然事物:天、地、山、泽[3]、雷、风、水及火。这八卦互相配合,可以变成六十四个图案,每个图案都有文字解释,说明不同的人生状况。

GLOSSARY

1 避邪　to ward off evil spirits　　2 占卜　to tell fortune
3 泽　　a lake; a pond

Translation

❶ What are the Eight Trigrams *(bagua)*?

A small octagonal mirror can often be found hanging outside the houses of some Chinese people. This is not a piece of decoration. This mirror is called the *bagua jing* (*jing* means a mirror), which is used to drive away evil spirits. The patterns surrounding the mirror are formed from straight lines. These patterns are called *bagua*. Don't think lightly of these patterns, as they represent the important philosophical thinking of the Chinese people.

According to legends the *bagua* was drawn by the Chinese ancestor, *Fuxi*. Later on t he eight patterns in the *bagua* were recorded in *I Ching*, which is the oldest Chinese fortune-telling book. The *bagua* is used to tell fortunes. According to *I Ching*, everything in the world is changing. People should pay attention to changes. The Chinese character, "*I*" means to change. It should be pronounced in the context when it means "to change" and not in the context meaning "easy".

According to Confucius's interpretation of the Book of Change, *I Ching* the world was originally one gaseous body, which mutated into two values, the yin and the yang. From these two values, the yin and the yang four phenomena can be derived. From the four phenomena eight patterns have been created and these eight patterns constitute the *bagua*, the eight patterns of which can represent eight natural phenomena, namely Heaven, Earth, Mountain, Lake, Thunder, Wind, Water and Fire. From the mutual multiplication of these eight patterns (each as a unit) they can become 64 different patterns, each of which has its own written illustrations and interpretations of the different situations people encounter in life.

❷ 八卦和中国人的思想

《易经》对中国的文化和中国人的思想影响很大。中国的思想家孔子也曾用《易经》来教学。《易经》虽然是占卜的书，可是《易经》不会说明事情的结果。《易经》分析事物的状况，帮助人判断怎样使事情变得更好。古时候，人们打仗前会先占卜，再决定对策[4]。当然，每个人都希望人生[5]顺利，不会遇到困难和危险。不过，生命里有吉[6]也有凶[7]，好比有晴天，也有雨天。中国人相信，人无法避免自然的灾害，但可以减少人造成的危机。什么人的凶比较多？要是一个人做了坏事，会担心有人发现。他的危机当然比较多，因此也不快乐。一个没有做坏

事 的 人， 就 没有
这些 担心。 什么 人
的 吉 比较 多？ 如果
你 很 喜欢 帮助 人，
有 困难 的 时候， 也
会 有 人 帮助 你。
所以， 就算[8] 遇到
危机， 也 比较 容易 解决。
《易经》不但 可以 用 来 占卜， 也 教导
我们 对待 别人 的 态度 和 处理 事情 的
方法。

Confucius

GLOSSARY

4 对策　strategy
5 人生　life
6 吉　good luck
7 凶　back luck
8 就算　even if, even though

47

Translation

❷ The *Bagua* and the Philosophical Thinking of the Chinese People

    The culture of the Chinese and the philosophical thinking of the Chinese people have been greatly influenced by the Book of Change, *I Ching*. Confucius, a Chinese thinker also used the Book of Change, *I Ching* to teach in his career as an educator. Although the Book of Change, *I Ching* is a book used for fortune telling, it will not explicitly illustrate the outcome of an event. *I Ching* can be used to analyze the situation of an event and the analysis can be used to help people decide what to do in order to make the changes so that the outcome of the event can be better. In ancient times before fighting a battle people would use *I Ching* to tell fortunes. Then they decided on a strategic plan. Of course everyone hopes to have an easy life, in which he or she will never encounter any difficulty or danger. But just like our daily weather, which can be sunny or rainy, there are lucky occasions and dangerous situations in one's life. Chinese people believe that no one can avoid the occurrence of natural disasters but risky conditions caused by the people can be reduced. What kind of people is more likely to have bad luck? People who have done bad deeds always worry that their wrong doings will be discovered. As a result the risks of bad luck falling on them will increase. Therefore they will never be happy. If a person has never done any bad deed he or she will never have this kind of worry. What kind of people will increase their chances of meeting good fortune? If you love to help people, people will also help you in return. It will be easier for you to deal with a crisis if you happen to encounter one.

    I Ching is not only a book used for fortune telling, it also teaches the manner and attitude for treating other people and the way of managing one' affairs.

❸ 八卦 和 应用

风水学 是 最 常见 的 八卦 应用。北京 的 天坛、地坛、日坛 与 月坛，就是 按照 八卦 的 原理 建造 的。八卦 的 八 种 自然现象，分别 分布 在 八 个 位置 和 方向 上。而 天、地、日、月坛 就 正好 在 南、北、东、西方，配合 了 八卦 的 位置 和 方向。

The Temple of Heaven

Zhōngguórén hěn zhòngshì jiànzhùwù de dìdiǎn, yīnwèi
中国人 很 重视 建筑物 的 地点, 因为
tāmen xiāngxìn rén huì shòu huánjìng de yǐngxiǎng. Rúguǒ
他们 相信 人 会 受 环境 的 影响。 如果
jiànzhùwù hé huánjìng nénggòu pèihé, biàn shì zuì lǐxiǎng
建筑物 和 环境 能够 配合, 便 是 最 理想
de. Rúguǒ nǐ de fángzi kěyǐ kàn dào shān, yòu
的。 如果 你 的 房子 可以 看 到 山, 又
kěyǐ kàn dào hǎi, xīnqíng bǐjiào shūchàng, fēngshuǐ dāngrán
可以 看 到 海, 心情 比较 舒畅, 风水 当然
bǐjiào hǎo.
比较 好。
Chúle jiànzhùwù, fàng jiājù de wèizhi yě kěyǐ
除了 建筑物, 放 家具 的 位置 也 可以

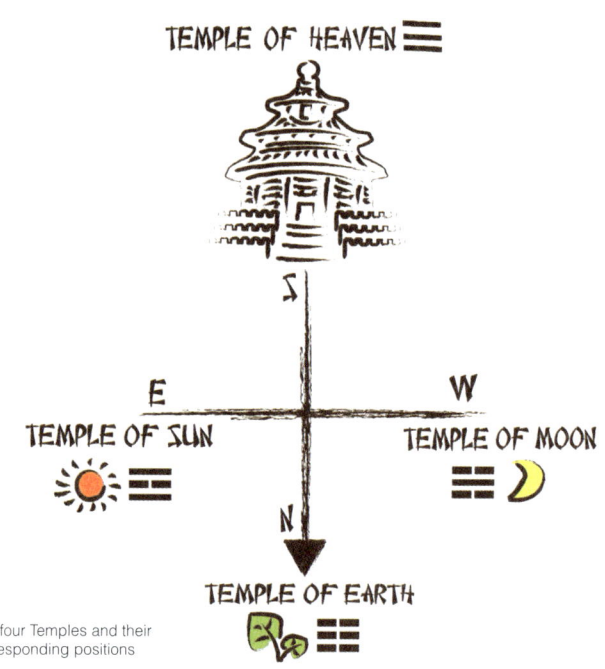

The four Temples and their corresponding positions

cānkǎo	bāguà	de	wèizhi	hé	fāngxiàng		bùtóng	de	wèizhi
参考	八卦	的	位置	和	方向。		不同	的	位置

和方向，代表不同方面的运气。中国人相信，家具的位置和方向配合得好，人在房子里就会住得舒服，运气也会变好。另外，中国人也认为，人也有属于自己的位置。每个人都应该尽力做好自己的事情，不要贪图[9]别人的东西，这样才是正确的态度。

GLOSSARY

9 贪图 to covet

Translation

❸ The *Bagua* and its Applications

The *bagua* sees its most frequent application in geomancy (literally meaning the study of the Wind and the Water). The four famous shrines of Beijing Tiantan (Temple of Heaven), Ditan (Temple of Earth), Ritan (Temple of Sun) and the Yuetan (Temple of Moon) were built according to the theories of the *bagua*. The eight patterns of the *bagua*, symbolizing the eight natural phenomena were placed into a distributional pattern of positions and directions that corresponded to the theories of the *bagua*. The Tiantan, the Ditan, the Ritan and the Yuetan were constructed so that they were in line with the complementary positions and directions according to the theories of the *bagua*. The Tiantan (Heaven) was built in the south; the Ditan (the Earth), the north; the Ritan (the Sun), the east; the Yuetan (the Moon), the west.

Chinese people put a very heavy emphasis on the location of a building because they believe that people can be affected by the environment. A building should be in keeping with its environment. If you can see the mountain and the ocean from your house you will feel more comfortable, because it will foster good "*fengshui*".

As well as in architecture, the theories of the *bagua* can also be used as a reference guide for positioning your furniture. Different locations and directions represent different aspects of fortune. Chinese people believe that when the positioning of the various pieces of the furniture complement each other, people will live comfortably in that house and their fortune will change for the better. Moreover, they also think that everyone has his or her own status in life. Everyone should try his or her best to do well in his or her own business. No one should covet things belonging to other people. This is the correct attitude in life.

The Different Dual Combinations (called *Guaxiang* 卦象 in Chinese) Formed from the Eight Trigrams?

The Eight Trigrams are formed from one basic unit, called *yao* 爻, which is a variable with two values, the *yinyao* 阴爻 and the *yangyao* 阳爻. Here we can respectively imagine them to be a lady and a gentleman (as shown in the diagram).

The *yinyao* is the broken line and the *yangyao* is the straight line.

Each *guaxiang* is formed by six *yao*. The three inferior ones are grouped together as the internal trigram (called *neigua* 内卦 in Chinese). The three superior ones are combined to form the external trigram (called *waigua* 外卦 in Chinese).

When interpreting a *guaxiang*, the most inferior one, called the first *yao*, is to be examined first. The rest of the five *yao* are examined in base-to-top-order, starting from the first *yao* and going upward to the uppermost one. The internal trigram is examined before the external trigram. The rationale of this order of examination is based on the Chinese belief that all changes begin from the foundation and individual personal behavior is affected by influences from within.

The Chinese think that odd numbers belong to the yang and even numbers belong to the yin. Therefore, the most suitable combination is when a gentleman, placed at the position of the first, third and the fifth *yao*, is matched up with a lady, placed in the position of the second, fourth and the sixth *yao*. Because of the traditional Chinese belief of the superiority of the male and the inferiority of the female, it is regarded as reasonable to place the gentleman before the lady. Moreover, because the alternative placement order of a gentleman followed by a lady corresponds to a complementary *yin-yang* combination, each being put into a suitable position, this fosters harmonious relationships. Therefore, a *guaxiang* fulfilling these requirements is one, which will bring very good fortune. If a *guaxiang* indicates two gentlemen or two ladies being placed together, they are going to quarrel and therefore it is not a good combination.

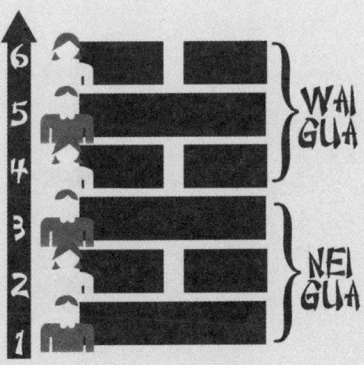

Hóng shuāng xǐ

红双囍

Double Happiness

Pre-reading Questions

1. In the picture symbol 囍 what the maximum number of Chinese characters that you can find? Are these Chinese characters related to囍?
2. Why is this picture symbol always red in color?
3. Why does it (囍) need to be composed of two Chinese characters with the same meaning of happiness? Hasn't one喜 expressed the state of being happy already?

Shuāng xǐ de gùshi

❶ 双喜的故事

zài Zhōngguórén de chuántǒng hūnlǐ shang nǐ huì
在中国人的传统婚礼[1]上，你会

jiàn dào hěn duō hóngsè de xǐ jiù xiàng liǎng gè
见到很多红色的“囍”，就像两个

xǐ zì fàng zài yīqǐ Tā shì bu shì niàn xǐ xǐ
“喜”字放在一起。它是不是念喜喜

ne Qíshí xǐ yě niàn xǐ Tā shì yī gè
呢？其实，“囍”也念“喜”。它是一个

图符,由两个"喜"字组成。

关于贴双囍传统的由来,流传着一个故事。

中国北宋(公元960年至1127年),有一个叫王安石的人。他去考试的路上,看见一对未完成的对联[2],是一个女子写的。如果有人能完成另外一半,女子就会嫁给他。王安石赶着去考试,只好放弃。考试的题目居然也是对联,题目的一半与女子写的一半正好配合。王安石便用女子的对联作为

A double happiness cake

Double happiness magnets

答案。考完试,王安石回去女子家,用考试的题目完成对联,女子便答应做他的妻子。结婚那天,王安石知道自己考试得了第一名,高兴极了!他一口气³在红纸上写了两个"喜"字,贴在门上。代表两件喜事同时发生。

从此,在婚礼上贴红双囍的习惯就在民间传开了。

Double happiness decoration at a wedding banquet

GLOSSARY

1 婚礼　wedding ceremony
2 对联　a couplet (usually antithetical)
3 一口气　without a break ; in one breath

Translation

❶ The Story of Double Happiness

At a traditional Chinese wedding, you will always find a lot of red double happiness which is essentially two Chinese "*xi*" (happiness) characters being put together. Is it pronounced as "*xixi*" (happiness happiness)? Actually, double happiness is also pronounced as "*xi*"(happiness). It is a symbol simply made up of two happinesses.

With regard to the origin of pasting the double happiness on red paper, there is a story that circulates among Chinese people.

In the Northern Song Dynasty (960–1127 A.D.), there was a man called Wang Anshi. On his way to take an examination (for his job as a government official), he saw an incomplete antithetical couplet. It was written by a lady who promised that, if anyone was able to complete the other half of the couplet, she would marry him. Since he needed to hurry on with his journey to take the examination, Wang Anshi had to give up. It so happened that the examination question was also to complete an antithetical couplet and, what's more, the half of the couplet in the question exactly matched with the line written by the lady! Thus, Wang Anshi put down the lady's line as the answer. After the examination, Wang Anshi dropped by the lady's home and used the half of the couplet from his exam to complete the antithetical couplet. The lady kept her promise and consented to marry him. On the day of their wedding, Wang Anshi received news that he came first in his examination. He was very happy indeed. He immediately wrote two "happiness" on a piece of red paper and pasted it on the door. This indicated that two happy events came one after the other.

Since then, the custom of pasting red double happiness at weddings started to become widespread.

❷ 中国人与红色

中国人为什么喜欢红色的"囍",而不是别的颜色呢?红色是太阳、火和血的颜色,象征了生命。红色令人觉得快乐、热闹、健康。孔子认为红色是很好的颜色。

中国人非常喜爱红色。结婚、小孩出生、生日等令人高兴、值得庆祝的事,都称为红事。结婚仪式上,新郎[4]和新娘的衣服都有红色,特别是新娘,她

Wedding gift in a red box

还会戴红花、穿红鞋子。结婚当天,新房[5]的门上、墙上、窗上都贴上红色的剪纸[6],新人[7]的被子和枕头也是红色的。家里有人有小孩出生,有些中国人会送红色的鸡蛋给朋友,通知他们好消息。此外,每年春节,中国人也爱穿红色的衣服,并在门上贴上红色的对联。

Red bridal shoes

GLOSSARY

4 新郎　bridegroom
5 新房　bridal chamber
6 剪纸　paper-cut
7 新人　newlywed

Translation

❷ The Chinese and the Red Color

Why do the Chinese favor the red color double happiness rather than any other colors? Well, red is the color of the sun, fire and blood. All these symbolize life. The red color makes people feel happy, excited and healthy. Confucius himself also considered red as a very good color.

The Chinese love the red color very much indeed. Any and all occasions, joyous, or worthwhile of celebration, such as marriage, giving birth to a child and birthdays etc., are called "red occasions" (happy occasions). Both the bride and the bridegroom tend to put on at least some red items upon their dress at the wedding ceremony, especially the bride. She will put on red flowers and wear red shoes at the ceremony. On the day of the marriage, red paper-cut can be seen everywhere around the bridal chamber. They are usually pasted on the doors, walls, and windows. Even the quilt and the pillows of the newlyweds are all red in color. In addition, whenever someone in the family has given birth to a child, some Chinese will give eggs which are painted in red, to their friends, so as to notify them about the good news. Further, the Chinese love to put on red clothes during the Spring Festival each year. They will also post red couplets on the doors of their houses.

❸ 喜和囍

Nǐ zhīdao wèishénme xǐ zì
你 知道 为什么 "喜" 字
hé xǐ zì biǎoshì gāoxìng? Yǒu
和 "囍" 字 表示 高兴？ 有
méiyou fāxiàn, xǐ zì de shàngmian shì
没有 发现，"喜" 字 的 上面 是
gè jí zì? jí zìrán biǎoshì le
个 "吉" 字？ "吉" 自然 表示 了

Wedding favors with design of double happiness

吉祥。"喜"字的下面是个"口"字,代表一张正在笑的嘴。有好事发生,当然心情愉快、开口大笑。两个"喜"字并列在一起,代表有两件好事,自然更高兴了。"囍"主要是用在婚礼上,祝福新郎和新娘的婚姻长久,永远不分离。

"囍"用在婚礼上也很适合。因为结婚本身是一件喜事,同时还会让人想到另外一件喜事——生孩子。中国人都希望喜临门,喜事不断,接连发生。"囍"字有两个喜,正好反映了两件喜事能一起发生的愿望。这种对喜事的盼望与祝福也表现在送礼方面。中国人以钱做礼物喜欢送双数[8],有时也送成对的礼物,祝福对方喜事不断到来。

GLOSSARY

8 双数 even numbers

Translation

❸ Happiness and Double Happiness

    Do you know why "happiness" and "double happiness" represent joyfulness? Perhaps you discovered there is the word "propitious" on the top part of the word? Propitious certainly represents luck. There is the word "mouth" at the lowest part of the word, representing a smiling mouth. When something good has happened, the person concerned will feel cheerful and smile with an open mouth. When there are two "happiness" put together, it means there are two good events and of course this makes one feel even more joyful. Double happiness is mainly used at weddings to wish the new couple a long marriage and never to separate.

    There is another straightforward reason why "double happiness" is appropriate at a wedding. Marriage itself is already a happy event, but it will make one think forward to another relevant event -giving birth to a child. The Chinese all hope to have good things come in pairs, and that happy events will come one after the other. Since there are two "happiness" in the word, it reflects that two happy events can happen simultaneously or almost so. Such wishes and blessings are also shown in the giving of presents. The Chinese tend to give an even amount of money as a gift and, in the case of giving gifts, they will always give them in pairs. This indicates a wish that the receiver of the present will have inceasing happiness.

The Magpie and Happiness

In China there is a kind of picture on which a magpie(喜鹊)is drawn. The magpie in the picture represents a sign of happiness. Two magpies symbolize the arrival of happiness as a pair, simplified in Chinese as double happiness. Why is a magpie used to represent happiness?

A magpie

Since ancient times the Chinese people have loved magpies very much because their sense of alertness to danger is very high. Whenever they are facing danger they will cry in a loud voice, warning people to run away from the dangerous situation. The people of ancient China even thought that magpies could predict what was going to happen in the future and that they had the ability to protect people. There are a lot of folklore legends about magpies helping people or delivering happy messages.

There is another reason why the Chinese love magpies. It is because they are in love stories. Perhaps the most well-known is the story in which magpies build a bridge so that two lovers can meet. A man called Niu Lang (literally meaning a cowherd) was in love with a girl who was a weaver and also an immortal. Later on they were separated by the Heavenly River, each being forced to live on either side. They were allowed to see each other only once a year. Every year on the day when they were allowed to meet, a lot of magpies would gather together to form a bridge crossing the Heavenly River so that they could see each other on the bridge.

Because magpies frequently help people and bring them good fortune in folklore, Chinese people connect the two together. As a result ordinary people in the community produce a lot of paintings and paper-cut art about magpies. Magpies as a group have become the favorite mascot of everyday people.

GAMES FOR FUN

There are four Chinese Characters, Zhao cai jin bao, hidden in the following symbol. It means attracting the enery of wealth and treasures. Can you identify these four characters (in traditional Chinese) and write them out?

Zhao cai jin bao

Answer:
Please look at this picture symbol carefully and you can find the four Chinese characters, zhao cai jin bao 招财进宝. Quite a few Chinese like to put up this picture symbol on the wall during Chinese New Year of the Chinese lunar calendar, expressing the wish of ever unending inflowing of wealth.

Fú

Good Fortune

Pre-reading Questions

1. How would you conside yourself to be in good fortune?
2. If you have to select an animal to represent good fortune which animal will you select? What will the Chinese people select?

❶ 你(Nǐ) 有(yǒu) 福(fú) 吗(ma)？

和(Hé) 家人(jiārén) 生活(shēnghuó) 愉快(yúkuài)，你(nǐ) 会(huì) 感到(gǎndào) 幸福(xìngfú)；
爸爸(bàba) 升职(shēngzhí)[1] 了(le)，他(tā) 的(de) 事业(shìyè) 很(hěn) 成功(chénggōng)；朋友(péngyou)
中(zhòng) 了(le) 大(dà) 奖(jiǎng)，他(tā) 的(de) 运气(yùnqi) 很(hěn) 好(hǎo)。在(Zài) 中国人(Zhōngguórén)
眼(yǎn) 里(li)，这些(zhèxiē) 都(dōu) 是(shì) 福(fú)。也许(Yěxǔ) 你(nǐ) 会(huì) 惊讶(jīngyà)，一(yī)
个(gè) "福(fú)" 字(zì) 怎么(zěnme) 能(néng) 包含(bāohán) 这么(zhème) 多(duō) 意思(yìsi) 呢(ne)？
在(Zài) 中国(Zhōngguó)，很多(hěnduō) 好(hǎo) 的(de) 事(shì) 都(dōu) 可以(kěyǐ) 说(shuō)

是"福"。能吃到美味的食物就是有口福², 朋友请你吃饭,为你准备丰富的晚饭,有鱼、虾等好吃的东西,那你就有口福了。

能看到美丽的事物,就是有眼福³。例如:你有机会到世界各地旅游,游览北京的长城,欣赏日本的樱花,参观巴黎铁塔等美丽的景色,你就是有眼福。

长得白白胖胖⁴,中国人叫做有福相。有这种长相,就表示活得开心,吃得好,穿得好,睡得好,身体好,没有烦恼⁵。

读到这里,你觉得你是个有福的人吗?

Good fortune design on red packets

GLOSSARY

1 升职　receive a promotion
2 口福　gourmet's luck
3 眼福　the good fortune of seeing something beautiful
4 白白胖胖　look plump
5 烦恼　worry

Translation

❶ Do you have Good Fortune?

You experience such bliss to lead a happy life with your family members, your father has received a promotion and his career is very successful, your friend is lucky enough to win the big lottery prize. All these examples, in the eyes of the Chinese, are considered as good fortune. You might be amazed to discover that the word "good fortune" can be imbued with so much meaning.

In China, many good things are regarded as "good fortune". When one has the chance to taste delicious food, he or she is said to have "gourmet's luck". Similarly if your friend invites you to dine, and this friend has prepared a sumptuous dinner with delicacies like fish, shrimps, etc., especially for you, you are said to have gourmet's luck.

When a person has the chance to view beautiful things, such a person is said to have the "good fortune of seeing something beautiful". For example, suppose you have the opportunity of traveling to various places in the world, to visit beautiful places like the Great Wall in China, the Sakura in Japan, and the Eiffel Tower in Paris, then you are considered to have the "good fortune of seeing something beautiful".

When someone looks plump, the Chinese regard this person as having a lovely appearance. Such characteristics indicate that this person lives happily, eats well, is finely dressed, sleeps soundly, and is physically healthy and free from worries.

Now having read this information thus far, do you consider yourself to have good fortune?

❷ 什么是福？

"福"到底包含了什么好事呢？

中国人认为，"福"大致可以分为五种，所以有"五福临门"的说法：第一种福气是活得健康和长久；第二种是富有而且社会地位高；第三种是生活得安心健康，没有什么烦恼；第四种是喜欢帮助别人，受人尊敬；第五种是一生

A *fu* Pendant

平安，儿孙孝顺[6]。如果能够享受到全部五种福，就是最有福的人了。

"五福临门"是愿望，新年时写在红纸上贴在屋里。其实中国人只要身体健康，家庭幸福，就已经觉得很有福了。老人能和子女一起生活，有人关心，有人照顾；丈夫和妻子感情好，互相支援，没有冲突；父母很照顾儿女，儿女又懂事。这样的生活，已经很叫人满足。

中国人相信福是可以积累的。只要平时多做好事，你总会成为有福的人。中国人甚至说："大难不死，必有后福。"逃过大灾难，也认为将来会有福。

GLOSSARY
6 孝顺 filial

Translation

❷ What is Good Fortune?

What are the exact positive elements that lead to "good fortune"? The Chinese believe that "good fortune" can be roughly classified into five types, which is why there is a saying, "the five blessings have descended upon the house". The first type is to live a long and healthy life. The second type is to be wealthy, and further, to attain a high social position. The third type is to feel at ease, free from physical health problems and worries. The fourth type is to help others and be respected by other people. The fifth type is to live peacefully throughout life, and that the children and grandchildren are all filial. If one can enjoy all these five types of good fortune, he or she will have attained the apogee of "good fortune".

"The five blessings have descended upon the house" is actually a wish and is always written on red paper to be pasted on the gateposts or door panels of the house. In fact, so long as one is healthy and has a happy family life, the Chinese will consider this as good enough fortune, in itself. When the elderly can live together with their children, in harmony, with someone to care for and to take care of them, when a husband and wife are affectionate, able to support each other and devoid of conflict, the parents have tried their best to take care of their children and the children are sensible, the Chinese will feel very satisfied indeed.

The Chinese believe that good fortune can in fact be accumulated. Only if you do more good deeds during ordinary times, will you finally become a person with good fortune. The Chinese even claim that " one who survives a great disaster is destined to receive good fortune for ever after". That is to say, when one escapes from a disastrous calamity, one is said to have good fortune in future.

❸ 蝙蝠与福

春节时，中国人喜欢在门上贴上福字或者福神的图画。细心看看，你会发现福神旁边常有蝙蝠[7]出现。常常和吸血鬼[8]在一起的蝙蝠，怎么会和福神有关系呢？

原来，中文的"蝠"与"福"同音，所以中国人认为蝙蝠是吉祥的动物，会为人带来福。传说蝙蝠的寿命很长，有的甚至可以活到一千岁，所以中国人更觉得蝙蝠是福的象征了。蝙蝠都是倒挂着的，中文的"倒"与"到"同音，所以蝙蝠倒挂着，又有"福到"的意思。如果蝙蝠飞进屋里，中国人不会

design of bats with *fu*

赶它们，反而认为是福到了。

因为蝙蝠代表福，所以中国的蝙蝠图案都是可爱的，一点也不可怕。有时在房屋的雕刻，玉器⁹、花瓶或杯盘上都可以找到蝙蝠的图案。

Chinese bats design

GLOSSARY

7 蝙蝠　a bat　　　8 吸血鬼　a vampire　　　9 玉器　jadeware

Translation

❸ The Bats and Good Fortune

The Chinese like to paste the character "good fortune" or the picture of the God of Good Fortune on their doors. If you look more closely, you will find there are often some bats depicted side by side with the God of Good Fortune. How can bats, so often associated with the vampire, have any thing to do with the God of Good Fortune?

It turns out that the Chinese character "bat" and "good fortune" are homophones. Thus, the Chinese consider that bats are lucky animals, which will bring good fortune. It is said that bats have a very long life, and apparently some of them can even live up to one thousand years. This makes the Chinese even more certain in their belief that they are a symbol of good fortune. As bats always hang upside down, and the character of "upside down" and arrive are homophones in

Chinese, when bats are hanging upside down, it means "good fortune" is arriving. No wonder the Chinese will not drive bats away when they fly into their house. Quite the contrary, they consider that "good fortune" has come.

As the bats represent good fortune, those bats depicted in Chinese illustrations are very cute, and are not fearsome at all. Such depictions of bats are common in carvings within the house, jade articles, vases and cups and dishes.

The Custom of Hanging the Symbol for Fortune, Upside Down

Something interesting can be observed when the Chinese celebrate the Spring Festival during the Lunar (Chinese) New Year. They like to stick large pieces of red paper with the Chinese character *fu* 福 (meaning fortune) on them to the doors and the walls of their homes. The strange thing is that some of these *fu* papers are hung upside down.

Fu and the spring couplets

The truth is that the Chinese character that means putting things upside down (倒) is pronounced in the same way as the Chinese character meaning the arrival of something (到), *dao*. Putting the *fu* character upside down then symbolizes the arrival of fortune. The Chinese people in ancient China did not have this custom of hanging the Chinese character, "*fu*" upside down. According to legend, there was a Chinese emperor, Zhu Yuanzhang, who frequently disguised himself as an ordinary person and went everywhere in the city to carry out his own inspection. One evening right before the Spring Festival (Lunar New Year's Eve), he saw a picture that played a joke on the empress as he walked on the street. He became very angry and he put the good luck sign with the Chinese character fu upside down in order to designate that particular house. He went back to the imperial palace immediately and dispatched an army to arrest those who were responsible. After learning what had happened, the empress secretly sent people to put all the Chinese characters for fu on all the doors of the entire city upside down. When the army sent by Zhu Yuanzhang went to arrest those people they could not find that family anymore. Zhu Yuanzhang could not do anything about this. He could only let them get away with it. The common people of the city felt that the act of putting fu on their doors would bring them good luck and therefore they kept doing it as a custom, which has been continued until now.

GAMES FOR FUN

Can you guess the implied meanings of good fortune from the pronunciations of the following objects?

Fish
鱼

Deer
鹿

Flower vase
瓶

Answer:

Yu 鱼, fish. It has the same pronunciation of left over, the second Chinese character of the term, shengyu 剩余, meaning there is left over wealth every year and the symbolic meaning of never ending wealth that can never be used up.

Lu 鹿, deer. It has the same pronunciation of the first Chinese character of Luwei 禄位, meaning and symbolizing a high-ranking government job with a high salary.

Ping 瓶, a bottle. It has the same pronunciation of the first Chinese character of the term, ping'an 平安, meaning safe and peace. Of course ping as a bottle symbolizes that too.

Shòu

Longevity

Pre-reading Questions

1. According to your criterion how long is a life span that can be described as in the state of longevity?
2. Which fruit do the Chinese use to represent longevity?
3. From 1 to 10 which numeral is related to longevity?

---

❶ Zhōngguórén duì　　shòu　　de zhòngshì
中国人 对 " 寿 " 的 重视

　　Qìngzhù　shēngrì　zuì　zhòngyào　de　shíwù　shì　shénme
　　庆祝 生日 最 重要 的 食物 是 什么
ne　Yěxǔ　nǐ　huì　shuō　shì　shēngrì　dàngāo　ba　　Nà　shì
呢? 也许 你 会 说 是 生 日 蛋糕 吧? 那 是
ŌuMěi　de　xíguàn　Zhōngguórén　guò　chuántǒng　de　shēngrì　huì
欧美 的 习惯。中国人 过 传统 的 生日， 会
chī　miàntiáo¹　bāozi　hé　táozi　　Bāozi　de　xíngzhuàng　yě　zuò
吃 面条¹、包子 和 桃子。包子 的 形状， 也 做
de　gēn　táozi　yīyàng　　Yīnwèi　Zhōngguórén　rènwéi　táozi　shì
得 跟 桃子 一样。因为 中国人 认为， 桃子 是
chángshòu　de　xiàngzhēng　Shēngrì　chī　de　táo　jiàozuò　shòutáo　chī
长寿 的 象征。生日 吃 的 桃， 叫做 寿桃； 吃

的桃形包子，叫做寿包。

中国人非常重视长寿。因为人要有健康的身体和长久的人生，才能享受其他幸福。

中国人对寿的重视，也与古代的生活有关。古时候，生活条件和卫生环境比现在差，人自然比较容易生病。面对自然灾害，人也没有能力抵抗。因此，大家都想活得平安长久，也希望有方法可以延长生命。此外，在古代，年纪大表示有经验，所以重视老人。因此，中国人很尊敬老人，也希望自己能够有老人那么长寿，那么有智慧。古代人重视寿的观念一直流传到今天。

GLOSSARY

1 面条 noodles

Translation

❶ The Chinese Emphasis on Longevity

What is the most important food to help celebrate one's birthday? Most likely you may suggest a birthday cake! However, that is usually the custom of people in Europe and the U.S.A. Traditionally, Chinese people eat noodles, stuffed buns and peaches for their birthday. The stuffed bun is shaped into that of a peach, since the Chinese regard the peach as a symbol of long life. Peaches eaten on birthdays are called "longevity peaches", and the peach-shaped stuffed buns are called "longevity buns".

The Chinese put extraordinary stress on longevity because only a person with physical health and a long life can enjoy complete happiness. The Chinese emphasis on longevity also has a connection with life in ancient times. The living conditions and hygiene in ancient times were much poorer than that which exists today, and the people of that time were easy prey to sickness. They were also unable to resist the natural disasters that befell them. Therefore, every one hoped to live a safe and long life, and wanted to find some way to lengthen their existence. Furthermore, in those long ago times old age indicated a wealth of experience, so that the people of that time thought highly of elderly people. The Chinese generally respect older people, and they hope they will enjoy the same long life, and have the same wit as the elderly. The ancients' concept of laying stress on longevity has been passed on till this day.

❷ 长寿 的 象征
Chángshòu de xiàngzhēng

为什么 中国 人 认为 桃子 代表 长寿 呢？传说 有 个 叫 西王母 的 女 神仙，她 有 不 死 药[2]，所以 她 永远 青春，既 不 会 变 老，也 不 会 死。

西王母 有 一 个 桃 园[3]，里面 的 桃 树 三 千 年 才 长 出 果实，普通 人 吃 了 这些 桃，可以 成为 神仙。每 次 桃 树 长 出 果实，西王母 都 会 办 宴会，请 神仙 来 吃 桃。桃子 是 神仙 吃 的 水果，在 民间 自然 成为 长寿 的 象征。除了 西王母 和 桃，寿星 也 代表 长寿。寿星 其实 是 天上 一 颗 叫 老人星 的

Xiwangmu, Queen Mother of the West

星星。人们相信只要它在天空出现,生活就会安定。他们还想像这颗星星的形象是一个慈祥[4]的老人,留着长长的白胡子,右手拿着一根长长的手杖[5],左手捧着一个桃子。

寿星甚至还成为生日的人的称呼,每次有人过生日,大家都喜欢叫他作寿星。

The Star of Longevity

Peaches

Peach shaped longevity buns

GLOSSARY

2 不死药　immortal medicine　　3 桃园　peach orchard

4 慈祥　kind　　5 手杖　a walking stick

Translation

❷ The Symbol of Longevity

  Why do the Chinese regard peaches as representing longevity? It is said that there was a goddess called Xihuangmu 西王母, literally means "Queen Mother of the West". She had some kind of immortal medicine, which is why she stayed eternally young, that is, she would never become old, and never die. Xihuangmu owned a peach orchard, and the fruit would grow only once every three thousand years. If an ordinary person consumed these peaches, they would become supernatural. Xihuangmu would invite all the celestial beings to taste the peaches. As the peach was the fruit eaten by the celestial beings, naturally it became a symbol of longevity among the people.

  Besides Xihuangmu and the peaches, there was the *shouxing* 寿星, Star of Longevity who represented long life. In fact, the Star of Longevity was a star called "canopus". People believed that whenever this star appeared in the sky, life would be stable. They even imagined the image of this star as a "kind old man with a long, white beard". He held a long walking stick in his right hand and a peach in his left hand. The Star of Longevity even became the name we call someone who celebrates his/her birthday. Every time Chinese people have a birthday party or celebrate their birthdays, every one likes to call them *shouxing*.

❸ 做九不做十

在中国，给老人庆祝生日，称为做寿[6]。中国人觉得，能够活到六十、七十、八十岁，是很值得高兴的，应该好好庆祝。可是，他们通常会在五十九、六十九、七十九等有数字"九"的岁数，就举办隆重[7]的生日宴会。等到老人正式整十岁的生日，反而做得比较简单。这叫"做九不做十"。因为中文的"九"与"久"读音相同，中国人就认为"九"代表了长久，是个吉祥的数字。

中国人喜欢在有数字"九"的岁数做寿，也与民间故事有关。传说有个十九岁的年轻人，只剩一天寿命。他请求

Longevity in chinese calligraphy

神仙帮忙,让他活下去,照顾年老[8]的母亲。神仙同情他,在他的岁数前面加了个九字,于是他就活了九十九岁。中国人做寿通常会吃九种菜,也会喝酒。"酒"的读音也像"久",喝酒就是祝寿星活得长久。因此,中国人把寿星的生日宴会称为"喝寿酒"。

A Hundred Longevity, a traditional auspicious symbol

GLOSSARY

6 做寿　to hold a longevity party (usually for the elder)
7 隆重　grand
8 年老　aged

Translation

❸ To Celebrate One's Birthday on the "Ninth" rather than on the "Tenth" of One's Age

In China, when people celebrate the birthday of an old man, it is called "holding a longevity party". The Chinese deem that it is something especially worthwhile to feel happy when people live as long as sixty, seventy, or eighty years old, and that it is worth an extra celebration. They will often hold a grand birthday party when anyone reaches the age of fifty nine, sixty nine, seventy nine etc., But, when the elderly come to the exact end of the decade be it 60,70,80 etc, their celebrations will be much more simple. Therefore we call this "to celebrate one's birthday on the ninth rather than on the tenth of one's age." It is because "nine" and "long time" are homophones in Chinese. Therefore the Chinese consider that "nine" represents longevity, and it is a lucky digit.

The Chinese celebrating the ninth year of the decade in their old age also has something to do with a folk story. It is said that there was a nineteen-year-old man whose life was about to end in one day. He begged the celestial being to help him prolong his life so that he could take care of his old mother. The celestial being sympathized with him, and he added a "nine" before the young man's real age, thus, the young man lived as long as ninety nine years old. When the Chinese celebrate their birthdays, they usually eat nine dishes, and will also drink some wine. It is because the pronunciation of the word "wine" is like that of the word "long time", so that to drink wine symbolizes the hope that the birthday person (or what we call the Star of Longevity) can live a long life. That is also why the Chinese call the birthday party of the God of Longevity "to drink the longevity wine".

The Noodles of Longevity

There is a Chinese tradition of eating a bowl of noodles on one's birthday. This is called eating the Noodles of Longevity. Shared among the people of China, there is an interesting story related to this tradition.

According to a legend, one day Emperor Wu of Han was making a joke when he was talking with his high-ranking ministers. He said, "It has been said that the length of one's life span is correlated to the philtrum (which is the length of distance between the base of the nose to the upper lip). The longer the philtrum one has the longer will be his or her life." At that time one of the high-ranking ministers, Dong Fangshuo, burst out laughing in a loud voice. The rest of them looked at him in a very puzzled manner and they were thinking in their

Chinese noodles

hearts of how the fellow, Dong Fangshuo, could be so insolent in his manner and dare to laugh at the Emperor? Dong Fangshuo hurriedly put in an explanation and said, "I was not laughing at his Highness. I burst out laughing because this man called Peng Zu, who is famous for his legendary long life, suddenly entered into my mind. He had such a long life and lived for 800 years. His philtrum* must be very long and can you imagine the length of his face, which must be even longer, mustn't it?" When Emperor Wu of Han heard this he immediately burst out laughing aloud too.

Later on this story circulated among ordinary people and they really believed that the longer the philtrum the longer one's life would be. Coincidentally, the Chinese character, mian 面, which means the face, has the same pronunciation as the Chinese character, mian 面, which means noodles. Therefore, eating noodles has the auspicious meaning that one would be able to enjoy a longer life, which is symbolized by the long noodles (face) with a long philtrum, the sign of a long life. Therefore it has become a tradition to eat a bowl of the Noodles of Longevity on one's birthday.

*"Philtrum" in the text means the length of distance between the base of the nose to the upper lip. This longitudinal groove is called the "*renzhong* 人中, meaning right in the middle of a person" in Chinese.

GAMES FOR FUN

When you wish someone a happy birthday, which two of the following are the most dreaded taboo presents to give to the birthday person?

寿包：literally means a longevity bun

红包：literally means red packet

寿衣：literally means longevity clothes

钟：literally means clock

Answer:

寿衣 *shouyi* – Clothes to be buried with a dead body. In Chinese 寿衣 may literally mean longevity clothes but it actually the type of clothes to be buried with a dead body and is not some clothes used to celebrate someone's birthday.

钟 *zhong* – The Chinese character 钟's pronunciation is *zhong*, the same as that of the Chinese character 终, meaning the end. The term, 送钟 *song zhong*, meaning giving someone a clock as a present, sounds the same as 送终 *song zhong*, arranging a funeral for someone.

Zhōngguó jié
中国结
Chinese Knotting

Pre-reading Questions

1. Do you know how to make string knots by tying up strings? Which knots can you make?

2. What do you use the string knots that you have tied for? Can you guess what do the Chinese people use the knots, which they tied from strings for?

---

❶ Yòng shéngzi zuò de zhuāngshìpǐn
用 绳子 做 的 装饰品

Zhǐ chuān bái chènshān yěxǔ
只 穿 白 衬衫 也许

huì dāndiào le diǎn, jié shang lǐngdài
会 单调 了 点,结 上 领带[1]

zhuāngshì yīxià, jiù huì gèng hǎokàn
装饰 一下, 就 会 更 好看

le. Tóngyàng de, Zhōngguórén hěn zǎo
了。 同样 地, 中国 人 很 早

yǐ yòng shéngzi zuòchéng jié zuòwéi
已 用 绳子 做成 "结" 作为

A pouch with Chinese knots

装饰,叫做"绳结",今天很多人仍然会用绳结来做装饰品²。

古时的中国人,会用丝做的绳子结着漂亮的玉做装饰,他们将这样的结吊在腰带上,挂在颈上。结也可以单独做装饰,像中国衣服上的钮扣,就是结。结除了用来装饰衣服,还可以装饰用品,例如配在扇子、灯或笛子上。结的用途很多,渐渐发展成独特的中国

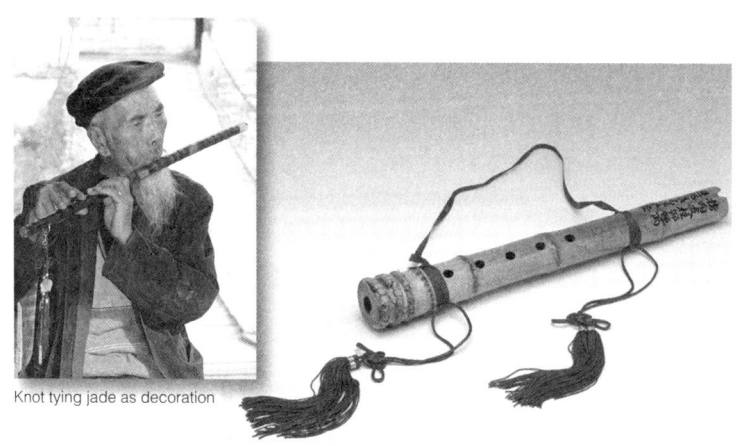

Knot tying jade as decoration

Chinese knot as ornament for flute

手工艺³,制作绳结的方法越来越多,结也变化出五花八门⁴的样子。清朝(公元1644年至1911年)的时候,皇宫里还有专门制作绳结的部门。所以,中国结既是容易学会的民间艺术,也是高级精致的艺术品。今天,绳结也可以做现代生活用品的装饰,例如做手提电话⁵的吊饰。

Chinese knots as a hanging décor

GLOSSARY

1 领带　a tie
2 装饰品　an ornament
3 手工艺　handicraft
4 五花八门　a rich variety of something
5 手提电话　cell phone

Translation

❶ Ornaments Made from Strings

Wearing only a white shirt may be a bit too monotonous. Tying on a necktie to ornament it will make you look better. For the same reason since early times the Chinese have been using strings to tie into "knots", used for the purpose of decoration. They are called "string knots". Even today there are still a lot of people using string knots for the purpose of decoration.

Chinese people in ancient times knew how to use strings made from silk to tie up beautiful knots with pieces of jade, using them for the purpose of decoration. They hanged this kind of knots on waist belts, and on the necks of the people. These knots could also be used all by themselves for decoration, like the buttons on Chinese clothes. They were in actual fact, knots. Besides being used for decorating clothes they could also be used to decorate other things, which people used in daily life. They could be fitted into a fan, a lamp or a bamboo flute. Knots had many uses. Gradually the art of tying knots had been developed into a unique form of Chinese handicraft. The different ways of making knots multiplied more and more in number. There was a rich variety of different types of knots. During the Qing Dynasty (1644 AD – 1911 AD) there was a special department in the Imperial Palace for making these kinds of knots. Therefore knot tying is not only a form of easy-to-learn handicraft but also these knots can be classed as high grade and refined art products. Today, string knots can also be used for decoration with things, which are used in daily life, such as the little ornaments hanging from cell phones.

❷ 中国结的意思

中国人为不同的结取了不同的名字,每种结表达不同的意思。用来象征感情的结,叫做同心结,表示两个人同一个心。古时候的人,会送同心结给喜欢的人。它代表两个人互相想念,永远不想与对方分开。虽然同心结表达的感情,不限于[6]爱情,但是后来常常用作表达爱意[7]的礼物。同心结也是婚礼的吉祥物,表示永结同心。它用来祝福[8]夫妻的爱情永远不变。因此,古时的诗人也将同心结写进情诗里。

Jixiangjie (Good Luck knot)

有一种结叫做吉祥结，中国人认为它有避邪的用途。人们相信吉祥结可以带来平安，使人避开疾病和灾难。

因为在庙里的帘子常常见到吉祥结，所以西方人又叫它做"中国庙宇结"。另外一个有名的结，叫如意结。如意的意思，指事情如希望中的顺利。

日本受中国影响，也用结做装饰。现在日本的庙宇，帘子上也有漂亮的结。

Chinese knot as decoration

GLOSSARY

6 限于　to be confined to
7 爱意　the affection of love
8 祝福　blessing

Translation

❷ The Various Meanings of these Chinese Knots

Chinese people give different names to different kinds of knots to express different meanings. The knots used to symbolize affection are called *tongxinjie*, literally meaning a knot of identical hearts. It bears the symbolic meaning of two persons sharing the same heart. In ancient times people would give a *tongxinjie* to another person they liked. It represented the sentiment that both of them cherished each other in memory. They never wanted to be separated from each other. Although *tongxinjies* expressed one's affection, they were not confined exclusively for expressing the affection of love. But later on it has been frequently used as a gift to express one's love of another person. A tongxinjie can also been used as the mascot at a wedding, with the purpose of wishing the new couple's hearts are always together and it is also used to bless their mutual love, which will never change. Therefore in ancient times poets used *tongxinjie* as a term when writing their romantic poems.

There is another kind of knot, called the *jixiangjie*, the Knots of Good Fortune. The Chinese people think that they have the function of helping people avoid evil spirits. People believe that *jixiangjies* can bring peace, and help people avoid sickness and disasters.

Because they are frequently seen on the screens inside the various temples Western people also call them the "Chinese Temple Knots". Another famous kind of knot is called *ruyijies*. The implied meaning of *ruyi* is to indicate one's hope that things will turned out as wished.

Because of the heavy influence of Chinese culture on Japan, in modern Japanese temples there are beautiful knots on their screens.

❸ 好结和死结

中文里有不少由"结"字组成的词语[9]。原来这些词语的意思,和绳结的特点也十分相似。有些是好的,有些是不好的。

"结"字的意思,是两条绳子互相连结。因此,不少有"结"字的词语,都有好的意思,表示建立关系。例如很多人一起,共同完成目标,叫做团结。一男一女相爱,决定一同生活,并举行婚礼,叫做结婚。认识了新的朋友,叫做结交朋友。

可是如果绳结打得太紧,很易变成了死结[10],很难解开[11],那就不太好了。人的舌头如果打了结,一定说不出话来了。所以,如要形容一个人

bùgǎn shuōhuà huòzhě shuō bù chū huà lái kěyǐ jiàozuò
不敢[12]说话，或者 说 不 出 话 来，可以 叫做

jiéshé Rúguǒ shuō yī gè rén yǒu xīnjié jí shì tā
结舌。如果 说 一 个 人 有 心结，即 是 他

xīnzhōng yǒu jiě bù kāi de fánnǎo shífēn tòngkǔ
心中 有 解 不 开 的 烦恼，十分 痛苦。

Yǐhòu nǐ yùdào xǐhuan de rén shí shì
以后，你 遇到 喜欢 的 人 时，试

shì sòng duìfāng yī gè tóngxīn jié nǐmen yěxǔ néng
试 送 对方 一 个 同心 结，你们 也许 能

jiéchéng fūqī ne
结成 夫妻 呢。

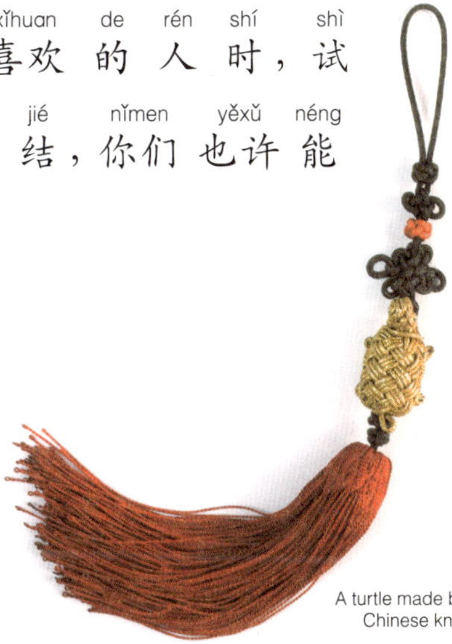

A turtle made by Chinese knot

GLOSSARY

9 词语 words and expressions
10 死结 a dead knot
11 解开 to untie
12 不敢 dare not to

Translation

❷ Good Knots and Dead Knots

In the Chinese language there are quite a few phrases formed with the use of "knots". Just like the special uniqueness of string knots some of these phrases have a good connotation and some not too good ones.

The meaning of the Chinese character *jie* is the mutual tying up state of two pieces of string. Therefore quite a few phrases, which are formed with *jies*, convey a good connotation of establishing a constructive relationship. For instance the act of many people gathering together to achieve an objective is called *tuanjie*, meaning uniting as a group. When a man and a girl are in love and decide to get married the ceremonial act is called *jiehun*, marriage.

If the knot is tied too tight it can easily becomes a dead knot, which is very difficult to be untied. That is not too good. When one is tongue-tied it must be difficult for him or her to say anything. Therefore if you want to describe someone, who dares not say anything or cannot say anything you can say he or she is tongue-tied. If you say someone has a *xinjie*, a knot tied in his or her heart, it means there is trouble or worry in his heart, which must be very painful.

From now on if you meet someone you like, try giving him or her a *tongxinjie*. You two may even get married later.

Some Common Chinese Knots

There are a lot of varieties of Chinese knots. The names of some basic string knots are derived from their shapes, their origins and their functions. Besides those that people are familiar with like the tongxinjie and the ruyijie, there are also a few kinds of common basic knots.

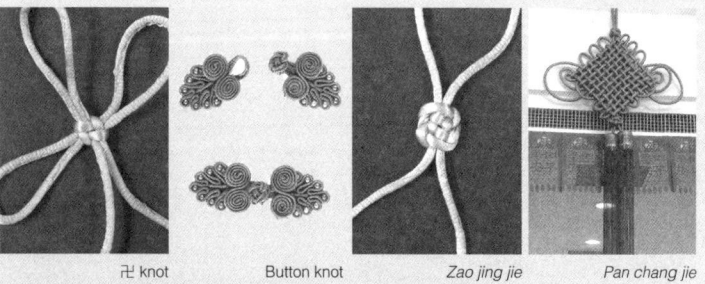

卍 knot   Button knot   Zao jing jie   Pan chang jie

The 卍 knots are knots tied up into a shape which looks like the character "卍". This character, "卍", is pronounced the same as the Chinese character, *wan*. It is a religious logogram of

Buddhism representing a sign of fortune with the implication of the accomplishments and fulfillment of one's moral vows in keeping the commandments.

The button knots : The button knots are named according to their function as buttons. But in fact it was only up until the Qing dynasty that they could be seen on the hats and crowns of the members of the Qing royal court.

The zaojingjie 藻井结: zaojing 藻井 are actually what we call ceilings today. In ancient times the pattern of painting used to decorate a large main hall was called the zaojing pattern of design. They were used to beautify the rooftops. The shape of the zaojingjie is like that of the zaojing patterns of design.

The panchangjie 盘长结: A panchang 盘长 (shrivasta in Sanskrit) is one of the Eight Kinds of Treasure of Fortune in Buddhism. It symbolizes everlasting eternity. The shape of the 盘长结 is exactly the same as the shape of the Buddhist Treasure, panchang. This is why they are called panchangjie. They are bigger in shape and are more refined in structure and composition. They do not change in shape even when heavy objects are hung underneath them. Therefore, they are often used singly as a unit.

GAMES FOR FUN

Please try to follow the pictures to tie a simple tongxinjie knot.

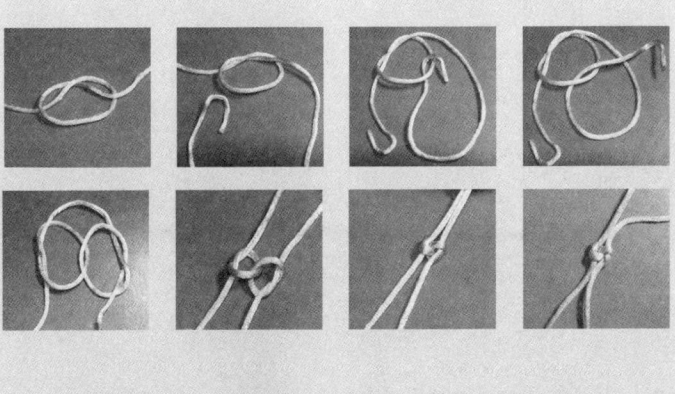

Mén shén
门神
The Door Gods

Pre-reading Questions

1. Do you put up pictures or decorations on your door? Do they have any special meanings?
2. Chinese people also put up pictures on their doors. Can you guess what are they being used for?
3. Why are these pictures always appearing as a pair?

---

❶ Mén shàng de shǒuwèi
门 上 的 守卫[1]

Zài Zhōngguó, lián pǔtōng lǎobǎixìng de fángzi dōu
在 中国，连 普通 老百姓 的 房子 都
yǒu shǒuwèi? Shìde, Zhōngguó yǒu ménshén. Ménshén gāodà
有 守卫？是的，中国 有 门神。门神 高大
wēifēng[2], biǎoqíng yánlì, duōshù chuān jūnrén fúzhuāng, hái
威风[2]，表情 严厉，多数 穿 军人 服装，还
ná zhe wǔqì. Gǔdài de Zhōngguórén rènwéi, měi
拿 着 武器。古代 的 中国人 认为，每
dào yèwǎn, guǐguài jiù huì chūlai huódòng. Zhōngguórén
到 夜晚，鬼怪[3] 就 会 出来 活动。中国人

相信,门神可以保护住宅的安全,只要在门上有神的图画,就可以吓走鬼怪。于是门神被画成画像[4],贴在门上。

中国古代的房子,大门是两扇[5]一对的,所以门神也是两个一对的样子。这一对门神都画成侧身站着,所以贴的时候,是两个门神相向[6],不能够贴成两个门神相背着。如果两个门神背向着对方,看起来就会像是不理睬对方似的。像广东等地方就有句话叫做"贴错门神",形容两个人常常闹意见,互相不理睬。

中国的门神的信仰一直流传到今天。虽然现在的房子常常用一扇的大门,但是每年春节,有些人还会在门口贴一对门神。

GLOSSARY

1 守卫 a guard
2 威风 majestic and awe-inspiring
3 鬼怪 ghosts and monsters
4 画像 portrait
5 扇   the measure wod for doors and windows
6 相向 facing each other; face to face

Door gods painted on the doors

Translation

❶ The Guards on the Door

In China even ordinary folks can afford guards for their houses! Yes, it is correct. In China there are door gods, who are big, tall, with a majestic and fearsome appearance on their faces. Most of them dressed like soldiers, even holding weapons in their hands. In ancient China people thought that when night came, evil spirits and monsters would come out to do their activities. Chinese people believe that door gods can protect their residential places, making them a safe place to live in. One only has to have a painting of the door gods on one's door, evil spirits and monsters will be driven away. Therefore door gods have been drawn on paintings to be put up on the doors.

In ancient China the main gates of the houses were built with the design of two doors. Therefore door gods also appeared in pairs, one on each door and two as a group. They stood sideways; one of the pair had his left side facing outward as the most anterior part of the body; the other partner of the pair was a mirror image of the other and therefore had his right side facing outward as the most anterior part of the body. Since they were painted individually, with one door god on one painting, one had to put up this pair of paintings in the manner that they were facing each other, not facing away from each other. If they were put up with their backs opposing each other it was like two persons trying to ignore each other. In many areas of the Province of Guangdong, (where the dialect, Cantonese is spoken) there is a saying, (which is pronounced in Mandarin as) *tie cuo menshen*, meaning the door gods have been put up in a wrongful manner, with their backs facing each other. The saying very symbolically sums up the relationship between two persons, who frequently disagree in opinions and always try to ignore each other when they have to be together.

The belief in door gods has been circulating in China up till today. Although modern houses are frequently built with the design of only one door, every year during the Spring Festival some people will still put up a pair of door gods on their doors.

❷ 门神的由来

中国有不同的门神形象,后来还发展到有女性门神。可是,门神的形象通常都是威风

Door gods on temple doors

的勇士。最早的门神出现在汉朝(公元前206年至公元220年)。传说很久以前,在一座山上,住着两个懂得捉鬼的兄弟。如果有鬼怪做坏事,打扰老百姓,他们就用绳子绑起鬼怪,捉去喂老虎。大家很感激这两兄弟,于是画下他们的样子,贴在家门上,用来驱赶[7]鬼怪。另外一对常见的门神,出现得比较晚,是两个唐朝(公元618年至907年)的战士。传说皇帝每天晚上都听到

奇怪的声音,还经常做恶梦,无法好好睡觉。皇帝认为是鬼怪打扰他,因此,他安排两位英勇的战士站在房间门口外守护他。当天晚上,果然非常安静,什么事也没有发生。皇帝不想两位战士太辛苦,便吩咐人画下他们,贴在门上,阻挡鬼怪。从此,皇帝晚上便感到非常安心。后来,这两个历史上的真战士就成了门神。

GLOSSARY

7 驱赶   to drive away

Translation

❷ The Origins of Door Gods

In China there are different images of door gods. Later on the images of female door goddesses have been added on as a new trend of development, Nevertheless door gods usually appear in the image of brave people with a majestic appearance. The earliest image of a door god appeared in the Han dynasty (206B.C. – 220A.D.) According to legends, a long long time ago there were two brothers who lived in the mountain. They had the supernatural ability to capture ghosts. If there were ghosts or monsters doing bad things to disrupt the peaceful living of ordinary folks they would use ropes to catch them and to tie them up and to feed them to the tigers. Everyone was so thankful of them that their appearances were drawn on paintings and put on the doors for the purpose of driving away the evil spirits and the monsters. Another frequently encountered version of the image of door gods, occurring usually as a pair appeared in a later stage in Chinese history. They originated from two warriors in the Tang dynasty (618 – 907). According to legends the emperor in that period of time heard strange noises every night. On top of that he frequently had nightmares and could not sleep well. The emperor thought that it was the evil spirits and the monsters that had been troubling him. Therefore he made an arrangement to have two brave warriors standing just outside the door of his room to act as security guards for him. Just as he expected, things were quiet on the very first night of the above arrangement. Nothing happened. The emperor did not want the two warriors to work too hard and therefore ordered painters to draw pictures of the two warriors and put those pictures on the door to block the evil spirits and the monsters. From then on the emperor felt very safe and secure. Later on these two warriors who really existed in Chinese history have become the legendary door gods that we see today.

❸ 门神与门画

因为大家爱贴门神,各地的人都画门神,门神也发展成为一种民间艺术。有些门神是直接画在门上的,也有些是用木头或者石头雕刻而成的。当然,最常见的门神形式还是画在纸上的图画。如果门很高大,门神也会画得很高大,有些跟一扇门一样高。不过,普通人家的门神一般都不高。

或许你会发现,有些门上贴的不是

Different forms of door gods

勇士。原来，除了将门神画成勇士，也可以画成官员的形象。不同的门神，功能也不同。穿着战斗衣服、手上拿着武器的勇士，作用是避邪，保护住宅平安。官员形象的门神，样子斯文温和，手上拿着官员戴的帽子，表现了贴门神的人希望富有和地位高的心愿。

从门神形象的演变[8]可以看到，人从本来单纯希望能够得到保护，发展到将自己的愿望寄托[9]在门神上。

Door gods holding an axe

GLOSSARY

8 演变 to develop; to evolve

9 寄托 to place (hope, etc.) on

Translation

❸ The Door Gods and the Related Door Paintings

Because of the fact that people like to put up door gods on their doors, door gods have evolved into a form of art in folk culture. Some door gods are designs used to be drawn directly on the doors. There are also some door gods' designs, which are carved on stone or wood. Of course the most common form of depiction of door gods is still those that appear as paintings drawn on paper. If the door is big and tall the door gods can be drawn relatively as bigger and as taller ones. Some can be as big and as tall as the doors. But door gods of ordinary people are usually not tall.

You may once in a while discover that the door gods on the doors are not the regular brave warriors. The fact of the matter is that besides being drawn as brave warriors, door gods can also be drawn as government officers. Different door gods have been created to serve different functions. Those door gods who look like brave warriors, dressed in military uniforms, holding weapons in their hands are used to drive away evil spirits and to protect the family and the household belongings, keeping everyone safe and sound. Those door gods who have the image of government officers look gentle and mild in manner. Each one holds a hat worn by government officers. They express the wishes of wealth and high social esteem of those who put up this kind of door god.

The evolution of the images of different types of door gods reflects the development of people's wishes from just getting protection to much higher expectations.

How Zhong Kui Became the Door God

If you ask the Chinese who is the most formidable and the best ghost catcher in China, they probably will tell you that it is Zhong Kui, who is also a very commonly seen gate-guarding god. There are a few folk stories describing incidents of how Zhong Kui became a gate-guarding god. One of them is like this:

According to a legend, emperor Xuanzong of the Tang dynasty had been sick for a month and there was still no improvement in his health. One night he had a dream in which he saw a small ghost making a lot of trouble in the imperial palace. This made him extremely angry. Then, a fearsome looking man came running to help. In a single attempt he caught that small ghost. Greatly surprised by his ability, Xuanzong asked the man who he was. He said he had failed his government examinations and cannot be a government officer. Later on he committed suicide. After he died he made a strong commitment to get rid of all the evil spirits, all the ghosts and all the monsters of the world as his way to serve his country. After the Emperor awoke from this dream his sickness was quite unexpectedly cured without the use of any medicine. He then ordered people to draw a picture according to what he told them he had seen in his dream, showing what Zhong Kui looked like and how he had caught the ghost. Later, this picture showing Zhong Kui catching a ghost began to circulate among the ordinary people of the community. Everybody was putting Zhong Kui on their doors for the purpose of chasing away evil spirits, ghosts and monsters.

狮子 Shīzi
The Lion

Pre-reading Questions

1. Why do the Chinese always like to put a pair of stone lion sculptures in front of their doors?
2. In China why is the image of a lion does not look too realistic as a real lion?
3. Have you seen a lion dance performance? Do you know when is the time that there will be a lion dance performance?

---

❶ 善良的中国狮子
Shànliáng de Zhōngguó shīzi

狮子称为百兽之王[1]，给人威风、凶猛的感觉。世界各地有不少著名的狮子雕塑，好像印度[2]的狮子像、埃及[3]的狮身人面像[4]，都是神气十足。中国狮子的雕塑却有点不同。它们颈上戴着圈，圈上还挂着铃,像只宠物⁵。中国的狮子是善良的。

为什么中国人会认为狮子是善良的呢?

因为中国没有狮子,只有老虎。老虎是森林之王,常常伤害人和人养的动物,所以中国人对老虎既尊敬,又害怕。

由于古代时狮子是由西方的人带到中国来的,数量非常少,当时的

A bronze lion in France

The sphinx

A Chinese lion

人很多都没有见过狮子,也不太知道狮子的厉害。佛教说狮子是好的,所以中国人对狮子的印象很好。中国的艺术家没有见过狮子,也就只能想像狮子的样子。所以,其他国家做的狮子艺术品,样子比较像真的狮子,而中国人做的狮子,则像是神话里的动物。

GLOSSARY

1 百兽之王　the kings of all animals
2 印度　India
3 埃及　Egypt
4 狮身人面像　the Sphinx
5 宠物　a pet

Translation

❶ The Docile and Gentle Chinese Lions

The lions have been called the kings of all animals, commanding a majestic and fearful feeling. In many places in the world there are quite a few famous lion sculptures, like the lion sculptures in India and the Egyptian Sphinx. They are grandiose in appearance. But the lion sculptures in China are a bit different. On their necks they wear rings that are even hung with bells. They look like pets, gentle and docile.

Why do the Chinese regard the lions as gentle and docile?

It is because of the fact that China does not have lions. There are only tigers, the kings of the forest. They frequently injure people and domestic animals. Therefore the Chinese are both fearful of the tigers and they also respect them.

The reason why the Chinese are not afraid of lions is that in ancient times the number of lions imported from the West into China was very small. At that time many people had never seen any lions and did not know too much about the great harm a lion could do to people. In Buddhism, lions were regarded as good. As a result, the Chinese had a very good impression of lions. Chinese artists who had never seen any lions could only imagine what they looked like. Therefore artistic representations of the lions by artists of other countries look more realistic. But lion art pieces made by the Chinese look like animals from mythology.

❷ 狮子传入中国

在汉朝（公元前206年至公元220年）的时候，中国通到西方的丝绸之路[6]开通[7]了。西方一位国王为了表示友好，送狮子给中国的皇帝作为礼物。从此，中国就有了狮子。

另外，佛教也从丝绸之路传入中国。中国人对狮子有好感，和佛教有关。在佛教的故事里，狮子是一种神圣的动物，代表勇猛[8]，佛教的神和佛常常骑着狮子。

A pair of lion bric-a-brac

佛寺的门前,也有一对石狮子。左边的是公的,右边的是母的。

因为信佛教的人渐渐多起来,认识狮子的中国人也越来越多。中国人相信狮子是吉祥的动物,可以避邪,也可以带来福气,狮子慢慢成为民间流行的艺术图像。

The stone lion at Tiananmen Square

GLOSSARY

6 丝绸之路　the Silk Road
7 开通　develop; dredge
8 勇猛　bravery

Translation

❷ The Importation of Lions into China

In the Han dynasty (206 B.C. – 220 A.D.) the Silk Road between China and the West was developed. To show a gesture of friendship a king in the West sent some lions to the Chinese emperor as a gift. From then on China had lions.

Also, Buddhism was brought to China through the Silk Road. The Chinese people's favorable impression of the lions is related to Buddhism. In Buddhist stories, lions belong to a kind of holy animals, which represent bravery. The Buddhist gods and Buddha frequently ride the lions. In front of the Buddhist temples there is always a pair of lions, the male on the left and the female on the right.

Because more and more Chinese believe in Buddhism, more and more of them have come to know about lions. The Chinese believe that lions are animals of good fortune. They can drive away evil spirits and bring lucky fortune. Gradually lions have become popular folk art images.

❸ 守门的百兽之王

很多皇帝的坟墓前,有石狮子,认为鬼怪见到狮子,就不敢来打扰了。后来,越来越多平民也用石狮子看守坟墓。

狮子也保护城市和家庭。一些城市和房子的大门外,会有一对石狮子,保护住在里面的人。不过,并不是所有人的门前都有石狮子的。因为造一对石狮子要花很多钱,所以以前

A pair of lion statue at the entrance of a commercial building

只有在皇宫和有钱人的门前才有石狮子。因此，石狮子也代表了财富和权力。后来，有一家在上海的英国银行，也学了中国人，在大门前面放了一对石狮子。现在，不少大公司喜欢放石狮子在门前。

除了在大门前，狮子还经常出现在日常生活中。在农历新年时，会举行舞狮，表演很难做的动作，这也是中国重要的民间传统。舞狮还分为南方的狮子和北方的狮子，但是样子都是可爱的中国狮子，不是凶恶的西方狮子。

Translation

❸ The King of All Animals as the Gatekeeper

In front of the tombs of many emperors stand stone lions because people think that evil spirits would not dare to come to disturb the tomb when they see the lions. Later on, more and more common people also used stone lions as the tomb keepers.

Lions can also protect cities and families. Outside the main gates of some cities and houses there are a pair of stone lions protecting the people inside. But not everyone can afford to have stone lions because they cost a lot of money to make. Therefore in olden days stone lions could only be found in front of the gates of the royal palaces and the houses of the wealthy and the powerful. Therefore, stone lions also represent wealth and power. Later on, in Shanghai an English bank had learned from the Chinese and put a pair of stone lions in front of the main gate. Now quite a few big companies like to put a pair of stone lions in front of their doors.

Besides being put in front of the main gates lions also appear frequently in our daily life. In the Chinese lunar New Year there are lion dances, performing hard to do acrobatic moves. This is also an important Chinese folk tradition. Lion dances are divided into the southern style lion dance and the northern style one. Nevertheless the appearances of these Chinese lions are cute and lovely, not like the fearsome lions in the West.

The Lion Dance

The lion dance is a folk performance very common in communities where Chinese people live. During the Spring Festival and other similar festivals the lion dance is always on the agenda to celebrate these occasions.

There are different versions of the origin of the custom related to how the lion dance was created. The most widely known story is the one about the monster animal called the *nianshou* 年兽. According to the legend, every year a monster appeared at a small village. People called it the *nianshou*. The farmers

Lion at Yonghe Lamasery, Beijing

were tormented by the *nianshou* because it ate up their crops. Then the farmers used bamboo sticks to make a fake monster and they added pieces of triangular cloth to make the body of the monster, in which they hid two people. The next year when the *nianshou* appeared again, the farmers made a lot of noise by banging on their cooking pans to accompany the fake monster's dancing movements. The *nianshou* was so scared that it ran back into the mountain and disappeared and was never seen again. From then on the lion dance has become extremely popular.

In China there are two styles of lion dance, the northern style and the southern style. The former puts its emphasis on the external appearance, making the lion look like a real one. The whole body is golden yellow in color. Even the pants and the shoes of the lion dancers are draped with golden yellow fur. The latter emphasizes the realism in the artistic expressions of the movements and the inner emotion of the lion. The lion dancers will perform acrobatic movements, expressing how the lion scratches, licks its fur and rubs its feet. Although there are differences between the northern and the southern styles of lion dance, nevertheless performing the lion dance requires a very high level of skill from the dancers. Today, on occasions like the Lunar New Year, festivals and the opening ceremony of a new store, Chinese people will arrange for a lion dance to celebrate the occasion. For Chinese people, the lion dance brings good luck and drives disasters, as well as celebrating these various events.

GAMES FOR FUN

Of the following two lions which one is a male lion and which one is a lioness?

Answer:

The one on the left is a lioness. The one on the right is a male lion. There are a lot of similarities in the external appearances of a male lion and a lioness as conceived by the Chinese artists. They differ from the real lions. Even lionesses have manes. Therefore it is hard to determine their genders from the appearances. In reality the clues are under their feet (paws). The lioness is on the left and is being places on the right hand side of the building and there is usually a young lion under her paw. The male lion is on the right and there is usually an embroidery ball being stepped on under his paw. The ball has the symbolic meaning of power and a complete, colorful and all-round finishing touch.

Yù
玉
Jade

Pre-reading Questions

1. Have you seen the jade ornaments that Chinese people wear? Why do the Chinese like to use jade to make ornaments?

2. When a Chinese person uses jade as a comparison to praise you what good personality qualities are they praising?

3. Besides serving the purpose of decoration can you guess what other functions can one benefit from when wearing jade ornaments?

---

❶ Měilì de shítou
美丽 的 石头

Zhōngguórén hěn xǐhuan dài gèzhǒng měilì de yù. Yù
中国人 很 喜欢 戴 各种 美丽 的 玉。玉
yǒu gèshìgèyàng de xíngzhuàng, yǒude shì diào zài xiàngliàn shang
有 各式各样 的 形状,有的 是 吊 在 项链 上
de zhuāngshì, yǒude shì huán xíng, dài zài shǒuwàn shang huòzhě
的 装饰,有的 是 环 形,戴 在 手腕[1] 上 或者
zhǐtou shang
指头 上。

在中国古代,玉还没有严格的分类。当时,古人认为美丽的石头就是玉。到了汉朝(公元前206年至公元220年),根据中国第一本字典的解释,玉应该有几种特点:它的颜色美丽,有温和的光彩;表面透明,从外面可以看到里面的花纹;敲它的时候,会发出好听的声音;它坚硬,不容易折断[2];可以磨出尖角的形状,却不容易割伤人。

玉是美丽的石头,令人想起传说中的五色石。传说远古[3]时代,有一个神撞断了顶着天的大山,天空出现一个大洞,危害人类的生命。这时,女娲用了有五种颜色的石头,把天空的洞口补好。后来,人们认为这些美丽的五色石就是玉了。

GLOSSARY

1 手腕　a wrist
2 折断　to break
3 远古　an ancient past

Translation

❶ Those Beautiful Pieces of Stone

  Chinese people love to wear various kinds of beautiful jade ornamental decorations, which can appear in various forms. Some of these ornaments are designs that hang from necklaces. Some of them are worn on fingers and on wrists as rings and bracelets.

  In ancient China when a clear-cut and strict standard of differentiating jade from other forms of stone was still nonexistent people of that period of time regarded any beautiful pieces of stone as jade. It was only since the Han Dynasty (206 B.C – to 220 A.D.) the special characteristics that distinguished jade from other forms of stone were explicitly described, according to the first dictionary of China. It should have a mild luster of beautiful color. It should be translucent externally. From the outside one should be able to see the internal flowery patterns. When it is knocked on, it should emit the kind of sounds that are pleasant to the ears. It should be strong and cannot be broken easily. It should be able to be polished into shapes with sharp angles. Yet these sharp ends and edges are dull enough that they do not cut and injure people.

  Jade is a form of beautiful stone. It makes people think of the legendary five-colored stone. According to legends, in the distant ancient past a god broke into two pieces the giant mountain that held up the sky, on which a big hole appeared as a result. This hole put people's lives at risk. Nüwa used this kind of five-colored stone to repair the big hole on the sky. Later on people have come to think of this legendary beautiful five-colored stone as the jade in real life.

❷ 玉的比喻

在中国，玉是美好、纯洁、高尚的象征。中国古代人用玉来比喻美好的品德。一个人具备了这些品德，他就是高尚的人。例如：玉代表坚定的信心和勇气。中国人认为，高尚的人应该勇敢面对困难，不轻易放弃，甚至宁可牺牲自己的生命，也不能委屈地生存。这就是所谓"宁为玉碎"，意思是宁愿做一块打碎了的玉，也要为正义而牺牲。

人的品德与智慧是要培养的，就像玉须要琢磨的道理一样。玉本来藏在岩石里，没有经过琢磨前，只是普通的石头。但是只要细心雕刻，就可以做成各式各样美丽的装饰品和器具。

中国有句话叫"玉不琢,不成器",比喻人和玉一样,要接受教育,努力学习,不断地锻炼自己,才可以获得知识,成为有智慧的人。

玉也用来形容给人纯洁感觉的女性。说一个人"玉洁冰清[4]",就是指她像玉和冰一样没有杂质,不但善良纯洁,品行[5]也高尚。

GLOSSARY

4 玉洁冰清 pure and noble; as pure as jade and ice

5 品行 conduct

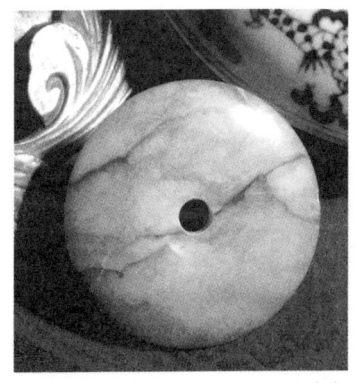

Jade

Translation

❷ The Analogy between People and Jade in Chinese Culture

In China jade still symbolizes the ethical merits of beauty, purity and high moral standards. In ancient China, jade was compared to people with these characteristics. Jade symbolizes a strong commitment to determination and courage. The Chinese believe that people with high moral standards should face difficulties with courage and determination so strong and so committed to not giving up, that they would sacrifice their lives and die in a noble manner. This is described in the saying, *ning wei yu sui*, meaning that in order to uphold the principle of justice one should be willing to sacrifice one's life. This noble act has been compared with smashing beautiful jade into pieces.

People's ethical standards and wisdom are qualities that needed a lot of education and cultivation. The same analogy can be applied to the fact that the beauty of jade cannot be observed without a lot of polishing and carving. Originally, jade is hidden in granite. Before the process of polishing and carving it only looks like an ordinary stone. But when it is carefully polished and carved it can be made into various beautiful ornaments and utensils.

There is a Chinese saying, "*yu bu zhuo, bu cheng qi*", meaning that people are like jade which needs a fine process to reveal its beauty. They need to apply themselves diligently in learning and education in order to obtain knowledge rich enough to attain the status of wise men.

Jade has also been used to describe the feeling of purity emitted from a lady. When she is praised as *yu jie bing qing*, it means that she is as void of impurity as jade and ice in their pure forms. Not only is she kind and pure but also her ethical standards are very high.

❸ 中国人为什么爱玉?

受传统影响,现代中国人也爱玉的美好含义。孩子出生了,不少长辈[6]喜欢送玉给小孩子表示心意;有些女人爱戴玉出席正式场合;有些女人平常也习惯戴玉环;有些男人会佩带[7]玉饰。好的玉,比黄金还要珍贵。中国人为什么这么爱玉呢?

中国人认为,玉可以保护人。小孩或老人戴玉,就不容易受惊。玉有实用价值,可以做成各式各样的器具,比如玉杯、玉盘、玉碗等。玉有保健的功能。中国古代著名的医学书籍记载:玉不但能

Jade pendants

使胃部、心和
肺感觉舒适、使
喉咙不干燥、促进
血液循环、使
眼睛明亮，还可以使人感到平静，不
会急躁。现在一般的美丽石头不叫做
玉。叫做玉的主要是软玉和硬玉两
种。软玉在新疆出产特别多，特别好。硬
玉也叫做翡翠，是绿色的，主要出产在
缅甸。

A jade bangle

GLOSSARY

6 长辈 elder; senior; elder member of a family
7 佩带 to wear

Translation

❸ Why do Chinese People love Jade?

Because of the influences of traditions, which have been handed down from generation to generation the Chinese people of modern times also love the beautiful implications of jade. When a baby is born, senior members of the family like to give jade ornaments to the newborn as gifts that express implicitly what they wish for the baby from the bottoms of their hearts. Some ladies love to wear jade ornaments to special occasions and formal ceremonies. Some ladies wear jade ornaments as a habit in their daily lives. Some men also wear jade ornaments. Good jade ornaments are even more precious than gold. Why do the Chinese love jade that much?

Chinese people believe jade ornaments can protect people. Children and old people will not be easily shocked by a sudden change of events if they are wearing jade ornaments. Jade has its value in practical applications, like jade cups, jade basins and jade bowls. According to the recordings in a famous ancient Chinese medical textbook jade has a health maintenance function. Not only will it ease the ill feelings of the stomach, the heart and the lungs but also it can keep the throat from getting dry. It can promote blood circulation; it can brighten up people's eyes; it can make people feel quiet and peaceful so that they will not become irritable and will not act on impulses. Nowadays an average piece of beautiful stone is not called jade. Stone that can be described as jade is mainly classified as two kinds, the soft kind of jade and the hard kind of jade. The former is produced in abundance in the Province of Xinjiang. Its quality is exceptionally good. The latter is produced in Burma.

The Origin of the Jadeite Cabbage

When you hear of this Jadeite Cabbage wouldn't you think of it as a kind of vegetable? In actual fact the Jadeite Cabbage is a precious jade artifact, carved to look like a Chinese cabbage. The natural colors in the jadite exactly match the colors of a green and white Chinese cabbage. It is 18.7 mm long, 9.1 mm wide and 5.07 mm in thickness. Moreover, there are two insects carved on its leaves. If you do not pay enough attention you may think it is a real Chinese cabbage. Why did the artist think to use a vegetable as the theme for making a carved jade artifact?
In ancient times the Chinese people thought that the Chinese

cabbage and grass worms were mascots. During the Qing dynasty, in the Imperial Palace there was a popular fashion of using various gemstones to make imitation plants, which appear to be the same size as the real plants. People "planted" them in their flowerpots, to symbolize good fortune. When the aforementioned Jadeite Cabbage appeared in the Imperial Palace, it was "planted" in an enamel flower pot and placed as a piece of decoration in the special section of the Imperial Palace, the Palace of Slumber of Jin Fei, a concubine of the Emperor Guanxu. Because of that, people speculated that it was part of her dowry. The white body of the vegetable symbolized the purity of her personality. The two insects on the leaves symbolized that she would be blessed with many children and a lot of happiness.

Therefore the Chinese people really love this Jadeite Cabbage, which has become the most precious piece of art in the National Palace Museum in Taipei, Taiwan.

Chinese cabbage

The Jadeite Cabbage